The Way the
Crumbles

Malcolm Kidd

www.capallbann.co.uk

The Way the Cookie Crumbles

ISBN 186163 152 9

Cover design by Paul Mason

Published by:

Capall Bann Publishing
Freshfields
Chieveley
Berks
RG20 8TF

Contents

Chapter 1

Something About a Soldier

The old doctor's hands were cold as he murmured 'Cough!'. Then he peered bleakly into my eyes, checked that I had no fallen arches or hammer-toes, asked if my hearing was all right, and then pronounced me fit to fight for my country, should it come to that. He said quietly, "You're A1!" Within a week or two I would be a soldier.

"Unspectacular" is about the right way to sum-up my Army career. But 'unusual', for in a way one could say that I started at the top, and then worked my way down! It had been a sequence of events which started with my boyhood asthma. From the age of seven I was one of the proverbial martyrs to the common affliction. There were few remedies then, apart from the well known "Potters Asthma Powder", a small quantity of which was put on a tin-lid and ignited. The ensuing smoke could clear a crowded room in a few minutes. Apart from that there was very little which could be done except sitting up in bed all night, propped up by six or seven pillows. And, of course missing school for sometimes months on end. Now there are very much more effective treatments. And it seems that most toddlers have their own atomizer!

In an effort to provide a more beneficial environment, I was sent to prep-school in North Wales. Each term I made my solitary way to Colwyn Bay by train. The first time I arrived at the little station I summoned the only taxi and arrived with my trunk at the main door of the school, in style. It created a minor sensation, but subsequently I did as all the rest of the boys did, and walked sedately behind a local youth who wheeled my school trunk the half-mile or so on a handcart and only charged sixpence! However, after a couple of years, as the hoped for improvement - as regards the asthma - hadn't materialised, I was transferred to Carlisle Grammar School where my absences were recorded in months, not days, and where I was always second from bottom of the class, that is until the other boy left.

With this undistinguished academic record employment prospects looked bleak, and permanent shortage of breath meant that I could do little on our farm, except that after passing my driving test, I was able to relieve my mother from the task of driving father in his livestock business, for he had never driven anything more complicated than a pony and trap. Then I stayed for a week with an aunt at Lancaster.It doesn't sound dramatic but it changed my life. Lancaster was only an hours' drive away-even then-but for some unknown reason the asthma left me! A miracle, no less, in only a couple of hours. After a splendid time I went home feeling that the miracle cure would be permanent. But sadly it wasn't! For I was just as bad as I had been before.So back to Lancaster again to find that somehow the air there, was what I needed. The magic still worked. I would have to stay! I had to find a job of some description and some 'digs' and an advertisement in the 'Lancaster Guardian' found me a job at the only thing I was qualified for; driving. So I was to drive one of the directors of a large building firm round their various sites within a fifty mile radius, and I was to earn two pounds a week. After paying for my digs, I had several shillings left for myself.

While the ominous shadow of war loomed nearer and nearer, I drove my boss around his multitudinous building sites in North Lancashire and in Westmorland and Cumbria. We 'clocked-up' a thousand miles a week. But my boss was an ultra-nervous passenger. And that is a very considerable understatement. I was never at any time to exceed thirty miles an hour! The boss probably would have felt better if he had been anaethetized.

Nevertheless in that first year we had three accidents,all serious.The worst was when a runaway lorry ran into the back of us as we entered the traffic in Lancaster town centre. If we had been travelling at more than thirty miles an hour we would probably have escaped altogether, but town traffic was stationary.

I managed however,to avoid an oncoming cyclist who was waiting for a chance to turn right, by the simple expedient of driving over an empty bit of pavement and through a shop window. My boss had no alternative and quite enough impetus - before seat belts were invented - but to fly over my head into the front seat. The other two accidents were all at low speeds, one in fact, when we were stationary. But he was somehow feeling more confident; I was told to travel at any speed at which I felt safe. But these two years of driving a nervous boss have left a permanent influence on my driving. And now it is I who is the ultra nervous passenger, if I can't somehow avoid being one.

At week-ends I took my home-made canvas canoe on the tidal stretches of the River Lune as far as Glasson Dock, and almost on to Morecambe Bay. Asthma was forgotten. Life was great. And I sometimes ended with a shilling or two for the 'pictures'. .

In the summer of 1939. youths of my age group - the twenty year olds - were given the choice of enlisting in the Territorial Army, for a four year stint, or joining the Militia Scheme. This was for an initial six months in the Army, followed by four years on the the Reserve. I never mentioned 'asthma' to the harassed medico and easily passed the second perfunctory Medical Examination, with the grade of A1, and opted for the Militia Scheme. The choice didn't make a lot of difference except that when I was finally called for in October '39. I was sent to a Territorial Regiment in Manchester many of whose members had joined the Terriers, prefering that to service in the Militia! But if I had had hopes of promotion, it meant that there were no vacancies. At least, not for the forseeable future.

We were stationed in Belle Vue, Manchester, which of course, was a Zoo, a fact which our instructors often delicately mentioned in the course of their remarks. We "Intake"- about a hundred of us - replaced what were called the "Immatures". Boys of seventeen and eighteen who were considered too young to go overseas. They were all posted to Home Service regiments. In fact many of them saw action long before the rest of us.

Belle Vue was still open to the public and during the standard square-bashing initiation period we did our drills, often distracted by the long-armed gibbons swinging on the trees of a little island, or by curious members of the public who - like us - were having their vocabularies suddenly and brutally enlarged. Later, during that hard winter the ice froze,thus enabling the gibbons to walk to comparative freedom. Some of us were sent to further afield to dig trains out of snowdrifts.

A little woman was wheeling a pram out of the Hyde Road entrance one day when the bored sentry checked her."I only want a deek at t'la-al babby, love!" But t'la-al babby turned out to be a ham which had been destined for the Sergeants' Mess. We had short spells of leave from time to time, to be followed automatically on return, by having to report for an "FFI". Interpreted, this meant "Free From Infection" Inspection! The drill was that one reported one's return to the Orderly Scrgeant at Reveille, then automatically went on the "Sick Parade" that morning.

The Sick Parade, a motley collection of shivering individuals, some in the first stages of influenza, a few regular malingerers, and some genuine sufferers waited their turn for the M.O. I simply refused to exhibit my naked body for the sake of an old regulation which might possibly have had some relevance,say, in the days of the press-gangs. When my turn came, I said simply,"Very constipated, Sir!" Without hesitation the Orderly silently dispensed a couple of the dreaded "Number Nines". These had the reputation of being able to relieve a costive elephant. I gave a smart salute and then marched out, to dispose of the dreaded pills in the nearest flower-bed. Everybody was happy. The M.O.to get rid of me so easily, and the Orderly simply had to write "M & D", (medicine and duties) on the sick report,and for the rest of the day I could use the implicit threat of the 'Number Nines' to avoid anything too strenuous. The F.F.I. inspections, a relic of days when there certainly *would* have been individuals who never returned from leave 'unaccompanied', somehow just died out soon after Christmas.

Spring had almost arrived and the Regiment was about to start its perambulations in the U.K., a grand tour which actually lasted until the invasion of Europe in 1944. The first move was only to Clitheroe, but I was to report to 60 Div H.Q. where the Divisional Commander, General Cunningham, needed a driver. Before the days of computers, they had been able to ascertain my trade or profession. There I was, the very man they were looking for, a professional chauffeur! This was to be the high point in a totally undistinguished army career. From then on I moved downwards.

The general was an extremely pleasant man to work for, and I was hoping to go with his staff when he went out to take command of the East African campaign against the Italians in Ethiopia and Eritea. Ffoyles bookshop had supplied me with books on Swahili and Amharic which I thought might come in handy. But by the time they arrived, the General had flown out without personel.

After a spell driving Brigadier Bucknall, a fairly elderly senior staff officer, we heard that the nebulous division was to be split-up. Already! (Bucknall was later to be "bowler hatted" by General Montgomery in Normandy for not pushing-on hard enough in spite of severe losses). I was sent back from Divisional Headquarters at Bedale, to my own regiment now near Pately Bridge; north of Harrogate. By this time I had acquired a 98cc Auto-cycle and I rolled up to Regimental Headquarters, 110th Field Regiment R.A. on this contraption, somewhat hampered by two kit-bags, a large guitar, and a fishing rod. All this was stowed away, as inconspicuously as possible in the R.H.Q. drivers area of the billets. The billets consisted of an enormous pigeon-loft, fully fifty or sixty feet long. We were told that the long shed had never actually been used as a pigeon loft, but even so, it was difficult to avoid an occasional scratch, and the statement was never believed.

I was assigned forthwith to drive "Z" car. This had nothing to do with the later TV series, but the large letter 'Z' on the car's wing indicated to all in an artillery regiment, that it was the Commanding Officer's car. Maybe the C.O. thought it would be a nice throw-away line to be able to say "My driver used to drive

General Cunningham, you know!" Colonel E.Surrey Dane, who had seen service in the first war, was a nice old boy with interests in the steel industry. We got on quite well. He had a habit of settling himself in the car, with the newspapers, or dozing off for long periods, and never, ever, helped with the navigation. Quite often when I was the only occupant, the car would be saluted by bods who wished to be on the safe side.

The colonel would get in the car and simply say "Northern Command", "Otterburn Ranges" or whatever, and leave me to find it. As all the signposts had been removed by this time - to baffle any invading Germans as well as ourselves - this was sometimes rather difficult. I simply stopped the car without comment and studied the map until I was quite satisfied, and then drove on. Nearly two years later, just after we had moved over to Northern Ireland, Col Dane, approaching sixty, was sent back to his steel works in both his and the national interest and I became one of the small team of R.H.Q drivers. May 1940 brought the post-Dunkirk invasion scares.These found us 'defending' the entire Yorkshire coast from the Humber estuary, up past Whitby to Robin Hood's Bay, a 'front' of approaching fifty miles. There was something of Dad's Army about it all. We didn't even have a rifle apiece as we went on early morning anti-parachutist patrols. Our old First World War eighteen pounders in theory had to cover over two miles of 'front' (each). I seem to recall that at El Alamien, Allied Artillery averaged out at about thirty yards apart.

Fortunately the threatened invasion didn't materialize, and we passed the summer at Brompton by Sawdon, a pretty village a few miles from Scarborough. As a nominal Methodist I was one of a handful of Nonconformists in the Regiment. The Army is actually designed for 'Conformists', rather than Non-Conformists, and as a result - after the inspection of the Church Parade - when the "C of E's" and the "R.C's" had been marched away to their respective churches, people like myself, of a variety of denominations generally referred to as "AOB's" ("any other buggers") were marched off to the cookhouse almost as if we were 'defaulters' serving a short spell of being 'confined to barracks' for some minor breach of army discipline. One short spell of the worst chores the Cook-Sergeant could find for us was enough for me. I asked the Orderly Sergeant if I could see the Orderly Officer. Both seemed somewhat put-out by this unusual request. The Orderly Officer of the day, was a nice young fellow straight from OCTU, with his first 'Pip', and he seemed nonplussed with his first taste of decision making. 'You're sure it isn't just to wangle out of these jobs in the Cookhouse, Kidd?' he said, rather shyly, as if he didn't like mentioning it. 'Absolutely not, Sir!' I said emphatically, 'Its just that our religious life is being sadly neglected, Sir.' He looked closely at me to see if I was 'having him on', but my face was expressionless. And having ascertained from me that the 'nearest' Methodist Chapel was in Scarborough, he summoned the duty driver to take me - and some very recent converts to Methodism - to the well- known resort. 'But you'll all have to find you're own way back for the mid-day meal!' he warned. That was perfectly acceptable to us for we fully intended to dine at Jacanelli's establishment before returning. The well-known Italian was the Harry Ramsden of the forties! I'm not sure if we even found the local Methodist Chapel.

We R.H.Q, personnel were billeted on the periphery of the small estate at Brompton,and the local squire's mansion was used as officers quarters, Regimental Offices, and so on. The absent owner was said to be a Sir Kenelm Caley, a baronet who had done his very best to provide a male heir to carry on the distinguished line. It was rumoured that he was the proud father of seven daughters, at the last count.

One of his ancestors was said to have designed and built what must have been the very first heavier-than-air 'machine' to fly, at least fifty years before the Wright brothers! Sadly, this seems to be a little known fact. The first baronet had made a glider of sorts, and because he rightly believed that his portly build and weight would be too much for the flimsy machine to cope with, he had put his lightweight coachman into the thing and launched it across the deep little valley, just behind where stood our Nissen Hut!

The 'glider had actually taken to the air and crossed the little valley before crashing and virtually disintegrating. The little coachman, almost unharmed, had crawled out of the wreckage and promptly given his notice! However the contraption *had* actually flown.

We moved for a few weeks to Catterick Camp before we moved again to more homely quarters, about fourteen miles from Stockton on Tees. The three Batteries were in the villages round Hutton Rudby, and we of R.H.Q found ourselves in a small mansion called Skutterskelf Hall. The R.H.Q. drivers occupied the servant's quarters in the attics, and of course had our own convenient 'servant's staircase'. A little later we moved to Stanley, County Durham. Our Batteries, 197, 208, and 475, were located in the surrounding pit villages, while our Headquarters were in Beamish Hall, near what is now a sort of coal-mining 'theme park' often featured in many earthy television series by Katherine Cookson.

No member of the forces stationed in this area will forget the incredible hospitality given to the troops by the local population. I will always remember a convoy which came to a halt in the then grimy streets of Tow Law during the first flurry of what subsequently became a "white out". The subaltern in charge climbed down out of sight and studied his maps. The snow appeared to really mean business. But within about a minute, doors opened all along the main street, and women rushed out of their little pit houses with jugs of steaming tea and plates of scones they could ill afford to give away. That was real hospitality!

Most of the officers and sergeants and anybody else who could afford it sent for their wives to join them and found them billets locally, and Colonel Dane's wife was found what was deemed to be suitable accommodation in the local rectory. I can't remember why I got my first seven days 'Confined to Barracks'. Up to that point I had somehow managed to keep my service record clean. This had taken a fair amount of ingenuity, as when I had heard on the grape-vine that the Orderly-Sergeant was looking for me which of course was bound to mean trouble of some sort, so I naturally kept out of his way. But I was discovered, as he said on the Charge Sheet; “Avoiding an N.C.O.by hiding behind the cookhouse door”. When I was faced with this "serious breach of military discipline", charged, and marched in front of the Adjutant, I resolutely denied the charge and with a straight face said 'Yes, Sir, I *was* behind the cookhouse door; but having been on leave recently I wished to apprise myself of any Standing Orders which had been posted in my absence." 'There are no Orders posted there, Sir' objected the surprised N.C.O. 'With respect, Sir, there *are* Orders there!' I maintained. So someone was despatched to see if this was true. I stood there at attention, hoping that no one had bothered to remove the well worn, and well out of date copies of some previous unit's orders which I had taken the precaution of pinning there! But I found some difficulty in keeping a straight face, as I was eventually marched out - an innocent man.

I *did* get C.B. though for 'skiving' out of the early morning run which the Adjutant had insisted on for everybody on R.H.Q. I had rounded the first sharp corner of the drive, and then, before the Adjutant, Edward Bowers, who was bringing up the rear, came into view, I popped smartly over a wall, intending to go back to bed for half an hour. Unfortunately the level of the ground was very much higher on the other side, and to avoid being seen I had to lie down full length, in a large bed of nettles. When Edward passed by, he heard me swearing furiously!

It was an open and shut case.I had no defence and not unreasonably, was awarded seven days C.B. 'Defaulters' had to parade for inspection with the Headquarters Guard when it mounted every night. Our three Batteries supplied the Guards in rotation. Defaulters were naturally examined with due emphasis on spit and polish and blanco, and were then allowed to wear Denims for their two hours 'fatigues' in the Cookhouse, doing all the dirty jobs that 'Taffy' Meake the Cook-Sergeant could provide.

As the Guard mounted - every evening, for a week - I watched the ceremony from outside the Regimental Office with 'Z' car at a strategic point near the door. Guard and Defaulters mounted. The role was called of the defaulters. From where I stood it was obvious that a defaulter was missing! Consultations then took place. Someone would point to 'Z' Car and me, standing patiently "waiting for the Colonel to come out". Heads nodded in agreement.

Kidd must be on duty! They concluded that I was about to drive the Colonel 'home' to his wife at the Rectory. It was pretty obvious. The Guard mounted,and the defaulters were marched to their grimy tasks.

As soon as they were out of sight, I drove 'Z' car away to a private destination of my own for an hour or so. I had driven the Colonel home more than an hour previously, and nobody knew his exact location better than me! But I never told a soul how I did my seven days!

Chapter 2

Jimmy's Christmas in the Glasshouse

With a name like 'Scutterskelf Hall' I wouldn't have blamed an owner if the name of the old mansion *had* been changed. Regimental Headquarters had been there for several months, near Stokesley, and our Batteries were in three of the nearby villages."A very odd sort of name; 'Skutterskelf'",I thought recently,as I drove slowly past those once very familiar stamping grounds with two octogenarians, Charlie and Jimmy, who had been stationed there with me, round about Christmas 1941, and we couldn't find the place at all. Maybe they *had* changed its name!

It had been unfortunate to say the least. Jimmy and I were given Railway Travel Warrants to go and pick up two Wireless Trucks from a unit at Haltwhistle which was about to go overseas. It was the sort of job we loved. To see a bit of the world, in this country, at least. Through Newcastle, where we changed trains and spent a little time and all our money, before taking the mid-day west-bound Carlisle train. Station names were getting very familiar to me.

We reported at the unit, which seemed to be in a state of some disorder,and totally uninterested in us. But we picked up the vehicles, duly signed for, and without hesitation set off for my home at Lazonby, in the Eden Valley of Cumberland.

We drove down our Dutchbarn Field, arriving at the rear of the farmhouse,so as to be as inconspicuous as possible. We gave my parents a pleasant surprise as we stamped down the back-garden. Mother was overjoyed, of course, for I hadn't had leave for over a year, and she immediately set about feeding us to the best of her ability, which was quite considerable. And of course it has to be conceded that food rationing had very little impact in the farming community.

Some two hours later,absolutely replete,we set off for Skutterskelf Hall. We were at least thirty miles off our direct route,which should have been - we supposed - by Tow Law and Darlington. Very few Army Forms No 412, - which were intended to authorise every single journey - would have stood a close inspection. And the mileometers of vehicles were never checked, we felt sure. We felt absolutely confident in our detour,and made good time, whenever possible, on the A66 road from Penrith to Scotch Corner.

The trucks had powerful V8 engines and could really motor. We had never driven anything as fast before."Make sure that the tanks are full", we had been told," for they are really thirsty beasts". There was little traffic and we got over fog-blanketed Bowes Moor in very reasonable time. We had just passed through the little village of Bowes - now with its by-pass - when I overtook a horse-drawn cart and momentarily wondered if Jimmy, behind me, would have to give way to an oncoming small car. Then almost at Scotch Corner I began to wonder where on earth he had got to, for there was no sign of him. After waiting a while I set off to retrace my steps, as it were, only to find that Jimmy, in fact *had* collided with the small car. Thankfully neither driver had been hurt, but the damage to the vehicles and the wall had been considerable, and the leaking radiator meant that the vehicle would have to be towed the rest of the way. The usual formalities had been observed. There seemed to be no hard feelings. It was just one of those things. The lady driver reported the accident and subsequently Jimmy had to face a charge of dangerous driving in the little courtroom at Barnard Castle, and was fined £2. This trifling sum, however, represented three weeks of Jim's wages and as a concession, he was therefore allowed to pay it off, at sixpence a week!

There were more serious repercussions,however from the Army. Of course we expected the usual Army informal inquiry. Strangely enough, no one ever spotted that given that the accident had occurred on the A66, we must have been *miles* from our route! Jimmy, as the driver, accepted that he would be put on a charge. It was the normal thing. He got three days "Confined to Barracks". No big deal, we all thought. It might have been a lot worse.

Unfortunately the three relevant days happened to be Christmas Eve, Christmas day,and Boxing day. The Christmas dinner itself followed usual army ritual.The Colonel had provided everyone with a pint of beer. Three cheers for the Colonel! And some of the junior officers rather self-consciously served us 'other ranks' with our meal. An old tradition. Another three cheers for the Colonel! However there *were* teetotalers in the Army, and others who were 'not all that fond of beer with a meal' so it transpired that Jimmy, the one man we all felt quite sorry for - an unfortunate 'victim of circumstances' - was the recipient of a number of extra pints.

A middle aged N.C.O. - almost 'elderly' to us - a reservist of at least thirty-eight, who still entertained hopes of promotion to Warrant Officer rank had been the Orderly Bombardier - when Jimmy had been marched in to get his 'punishment' for the crash. The bombardier was entirely innocent of any 'malice aforethought', and had no part in the actual charge. It was just routine. But building up in Jimmy's mind was the undoubted fact that he had been the victim of circumstances and the alcohol had diminished his capacity to accept these facts with equanimity. He was naturally filled with a strong sense of outrage.

And as the said N.C.O.- still unfortunately just within earshot - went round the end of the table, Jimmy mumbled resentfully, "There's the bugger who pegged me, I'll bloody get him for this!"

Most N.C.O.s would have turned a deaf-ear to this, in the circumstances, and passed on, but this one sharply called on two men, two very reluctant men indeed, and marched Jimmy off to the Guardroom charged with "threatening an N.C.O." The Second-in Command, an old regular soldier, who heard the evidence, professed to be outraged. "In over thirty years in the Army", he said,"I've never had to try a case like this. Threatening an N.C.O.!", and sentenced Jimmy to four weeks in the 'Glass-House'.

This turned out to be Hull Prison, whose original inmates had been turned out for people like Jimmy, and possibly some who probably deserved it. Even Jimmy's escort had to 'double march' with him from the prison gate to the administrative offices. And, unless they were locked in their comfortless cells at night, Jimmy and the rest had to 'double', (run) absolutely everywhere he had to go within the forbidding walls. When a long hard day was over, Jimmy and the rest of them passed by - at the double, of course - a large heap of rusty buckets, and grabbed which happened to be nearest.

These buckets had to be presented for inspection next morning with all traces of rust removed during the night, by the simple but laborious expedient of rubbing them with a stone. After inspection the buckets were hosed down,and left in a pile to get sufficiently rusty again, to "provide an evenings occupation".

When Jimmy returned after his month's incarceration, he naturally bore grudges, which more than fifty years haven't altogether dispelled, but fortuitously the Bombardier's promotion ambitions had at last been realised and he had been posted to one of our batteries.

We were all - except for Jimmy, of course - allowed out to Stockton, on New Year's Eve and the waggon-driver said he would pick us up at "twenty past midnight', and warned us that - like time and tide - he would wait for no man. In the event I missed the truck! And, honestly, I can't remember why! The three tonner was just disappearing as I rounded the corner. The lads were already singing as it went out of sight.

There was nothing else for it. I would have to walk. It was only some twelve or thirteen miles from the pick-up point, I thought optimistically, But with the blacked-out headlamps of wartime vehicles it might be better if I could give some signal to any oncoming cars. I bought a packet of twenty cigarettes from a slot machine and got a light from a rather drunk man - being matchless myself, as a non-smoker, and hoped to light one cigarette from the other until I got a lift. Then I set off on the long trail back to R.H.Q.

I practised giving a quick draw on the cigarette, and waving the glowing fag swiftly from side to side, as I left the built up area and headed for Stokesley. It seemed quite a quite good signal which should alert any driver to my 'plight'. But nobody came. Not a soul. By the time I reached Stokesly the cigarettes were done. And so was I. It was three o'clock in the morning. There were still another two or three miles to go. I entered a telephone box in Stokesly and managed to get through to the duty telephonist at Skutterskelf Hall. Would he possibly be good enough to climb up to the drivers quarters in the attic rooms, and see if he could persuade a driver - any driver - to risk a court martial and get a vehicle from the waggon lines, and come and pick me up? It was more than a bit of a cheek. It could end up with glass-house for both of us!

I staggered along the very narrow winding road towards my destination. Without cigarettes now, but I thought that waving a white hankie would enable anyone to see me! I had it at the ready. Then at long last I could hear a waggon coming fast along the twisty road. As it approached I waved the hankie and shouted as I jumped for safety onto the grassy verge. He went straight on past me, so I waited until he found a turning place,and returned. But he didn't return, and after a few minutes I realised that, in fact, he had never even seen me! So I staggered on in the rain and eventually passed the astonished sentry who had already had a rude awakening by the rapid exit of Jack's waggon.I got up without incident into the attic rooms. Everybody was in deep sleep.

Except for my old pal Briscoe. We had had a sort of pact that we shared any little luxury, so I felt under my palliasse for my secret bottle of cheap 'port-style' wine. Filling a pint mug to the brim, I shook Bris awake to share a delayed New Year drink with me. He reached up for the mug and downed the whole lot! Then he mumbled something and went off into a deep sleep.

By the time Jack Ramsey returned from his abortive rescue mission, justifiably annoyed - for he had gone all the way to Stockton looking for me - I was asleep! So was Bris. But soon we were all awake listening intently to his ramblings. He was talking in his sleep.We listened quite fascinated by his drunken reminiscences.

"Yes, I always remember what my nannie used to call me." He giggled quietly to himself as if to a private joke. "She used to call me 'Clara Wettibottom!'"

He would never live this down, we thought,with glee. He was unmercifully ragged, by all and sundry. But he reported sick next day with bronchitis, and was duly hospitalised. After three weeks he was "Y" Listed, in the normal way and then went to a holding-unit whence he was posted to the Western Desert, where he got a nasty crack on the head, was in hospital for months,and was sorely troubled with the wound for the rest of his life.

Chapter 3

The Alternatives

It was on a Friday,early in October, when four of my neighbour's ewes arrived uninvited. They were oddities from the start, 'just like their owner', I thought. The strays were of a somewhat unusual cross. They were obviously out of Swaledale ewes by a Suffolk ram. They hadn't had their tails docked when they were lambs, and the tails were the only parts on which there was an appreciable amount of wool. This of course,was because in their itinerant life - mostly spent on other farmers' land - they must have left most of their wool on fences and barbed wire over a wide area.

I recognised them immediately as belonging to Angus McKay; one of my neighbours and I groaned at the sight, for we had had dealings with Angus before, many many times, as had our respective fathers, and - like my own father before me - I had never, ever, come out on top.

Good neighbours are important in the farming community. And especially in connection with field boundary fences which are, in fact, owned by and the responsiblity of, either one or the other of the two parties; and if one happened to be a neighbour of Angus, they were a recipe for problems, especially as it had followed a long period as a neighbour of Angus's father. In over fifty years neither father or son had ever put a post or a nail in their boundary fence.

But this was undoubtedly *their* fence, for which *they* were solely responsible. And to be fair, the fence had improved somewhat after the advent of plastic baler twine. It lasted longer than mere string. Sometimes the twine wove an intricate pattern where bits of old rusting Victorian bedsteads had been used as "reinforcement" and incorporated into the whole rickety structure.

But anyone's stock can stray. One of my own sheep strayed onto another of Angus's fields next to one of mine.These narrow fields close to the village were the last visible signs of the strip-farming of medieval times. The strips would have been used to grow small quantities of cereals, mainly oats, but with some rye. All for home consumption.The straw too would have come in handy for thatch, for villagers' own cottages. The grain would have been milled in the village, for even small villages would have their own small water-mill. Self sufficiency was the order of the day.

And for a fixed number of days the villagers would be required to work for the Manorial Lord, and do his harvesting for him. Round about the Norman invasion, the standard wage for a full day's work was a penny, a pint of ale, and a loaf of bread. Two hundred years later, with nil inflation,the wages were exactly the same. And the standard of living had changed not a jot.

But on these narrow fields during the next six or seven hundred years there would be times when ploughmen would forget the golden rules, and because it was slightly easier for the plough to 'throw' the furrow of earth 'downhill' on a side-sloping field than 'uphill', it followed that in the course of time the depth of soil gradually built up on the low side, while on the high side, the depth of soil became more and more shallow, until sometimes there was barely enough soil to cover the virgin rock.

Thus my boundary wall was only about two feet high on my side, but on Angus's side the wall was almost six feet high. This made it extremely difficult for me - single handed - to recover an athletic lamb, well fit for slaughter, which had found a way over the wall. So I rang, to ask if it would be alright to leave it there until Saturday when I would have Fred's help to catch the stray and get it back over the wall. Angus interrupted me in mid-flow, and said "Oh, you needn't bother, Malc! Its deed, and I've buried it!"

When I "gathered-in" my own flock for routine dosing for stomach worms, I brought in Angus's old reprobates to the pens and after completing my task left the four safely confined in a small shed from which escape was impossible. Then I contacted Angus, and told him where to find them. He sounded really appreciative. I'd heard it all before, but he did seem grateful as he assured me that, this time, he would pick them up 'pronto'.

On Monday morning, however when I passed the sheep-pens, I was amazed, and in fact, very annoyed, to see that that the four sheep were still confined in the shed. Angus couldn't be contacted. His phone was dead.'Maybe cut off', I thought uncharitably. So I opened the door and let the old devils out into my field -'to save their lives'.

The Swaledale crosses had joined my flock just at 'tupping time' in October and were duly the first recipients of the attentions of my newly bought pedigree Suffolk ram. The ram - "tup" in local parlance - had been bought for a slightly smaller price than might otherwise have been the case, when I had bought it at our local auction at the annual tup-sale the previous Saturday.

Norman,was the auctioneer again. Thirty years before, he had tried to sell my army Bedford truck at my sister's farm sale. It was the same type of Bedford fifteen hundredweight with which I had grown familiar in the Army. But I had never realised then that it only 'did' about nine miles to the gallon, and had decided that because of this it would have to go. So it was entered in the sale. As we approached it in the long line of machinery, Norman quietly asked for his instructions. What was the limit below which he couldn't sell? The instructions I gave him were quite clear and unequivocal; "Not a penny under ninety pounds!"

He gave the spiel about the truck,and was very good at it.Then he asked for bids and quickly got one, It was only "Fifty pounds!" but it was a start, and without delay the bidding steadily rose to eighty five pounds, at which point Norman suddenly announced that the vehicle hadn't reached its reserve and they would therefore pass on to the next lot.

When I got the chance later I was a bit reproachful. "I wish now you'd taken that bid, Norman!" I said. "After all it was only a fiver less than the ninety pounds I'd suggested!" Norman looked at me a trifle pityingly. "I hadn't had a single bid!" he said.

When the Suffolk ram I bought had entered the ring, Norman made an announcement about it, after a brief consultation with its owner, before he started asking for bids from the assembled company of would-be buyers. Naturally, before even thinking of bidding, every prospective customer wants to know certain information. How many broad teeth, for instance. This is important; for two pairs of broad teeth in the front of the lower jaw would indicate to the cognoscente that it was a 'shearling'; that it had been sheared once only and that it would therefore be about eighteen months old. In the prime of life.

On the other hand, if the auctioneer announced that it was "full-mouthed" - it meant that the animal was almost an old age pensioner. But if he said,"broken-mouthed", it meant that the ram was really getting on in years; there would be gaps in the lower front teeth (in point of fact there are *no* front teeth in the upper gums of ruminants, just gums!) and that the buyer had 'better beware'. But for a small flock of ewes, say no more than thirty, he might be able 'to manage'.

"Yes, gentlemen!" Norman had announced briskly,after having the little consultation,"Mr Baxendale tells me that this tup is full pedigree, it's a shearling, with four broad teeth, it's absolutely sound in every way, except that it has only one testicle, but Mr Baxendale tells me that he will stand behind it". Not a soul even smiled at this possibility, however helpful it sounded. It merely meant that there would be a guarantee of fertility, or Baxendale would take the animal back. I bought the tup and declined Mr Baxendale's offer of assistance.

Next morning I knew that coupling had taken place during the night, with all four of the old Swaledale crosses! Because of the tup's ingenious 'ram harness', I knew exactly what had been going on. All the strays had received the tup's attentions during the night! Slight fault or not, he had had a very busy first night.

Ram 'harnesses' have now largely replaced the old 'Raddle' which used to be smeared on rams chests so that the act of mating would leave a tell-tale red smear on the ewe's hind quarters. Nowadays the harness holds a block of coloured crayon which does the same job. Different colours can be used as the weeks pass by so that one can arrange for the ewes with the first crayon marks to be kept 'handy for home', five months later, as lambing-time approaches.

I was going fishing - as a boy of thirteen - when Father asked if I could manage to catch and raddle our tup in Red Brows field as I passed it on my way to Dale Raven beck. "Where's the raddle?" I asked, and was told that it was in a jar, partly hidden under a tree root near the gate."No problem",I said with all the assurance of youth. But the tup wasn't easy to catch, even with the tempting lure of a bucket with some rolled barley as bait. Eventually I was able to grab a handful of wool and got a firm grip on his throat, as tup and I rolled over and over. Finally he agreed that I was boss and lay quite still, both of us panting very heavily, and with me almost exhausted. There was only one problem; I was yards away from the tree-root and the jar of raddle. But a boy happened to ride by on his bike, and at my urgent request he handed me the jar.

Father hadn't said how much raddle I had to apply to the chest of the recumbent ram, which was beginning to get his wind back,and was growing more difficult to hold. To be on the safe side I put on all that was in the jar and released the tup which returned to the ewes at a trot in case his services were required urgently.

There was a poscript to this. When Father saw the ewes two days later, he said angrily,"They are like a tribe of Red Indians!" They were *covered* in raddle! Apparently I had been supposed to apply only as much as the bit of stick in the jar would hold! As the ewes were intended for sale shortly, the sheep had to come home and have a wash in the sheep-dip. It took several years for me to live the episode down.

During the winter, after the arrival of Angus's ewes, we had had all our ewes in the pens from time to time for routine attention; maybe dosing for worms, or treating a lame sheep which had developed footrot. Again and again I rang Angus to come for his sheep,'while we could easily catch them'. for they almost needed tethering. But Angus never came. There was always some excuse, even when I did manage to make contact.

He seemed quite content to leave them where they were, knowing that they were in good hands, as indeed they were, because when they lambed the next Spring - each of them, unaided, lambed twin lambs!. "It just goes to show!" said Fred, rather vaguely. It was maddening to find, later on, that my own pedigree ewes had only averaged 'one and a half lambs' per ewe, while the four Swaledale crosses had managed two apiece! So now I was saddled with twelve of Angus's sheep! They *did* extremely well; they were really thriving.as well they might, of course, for they were always the first to have their noses in the trough. They had settled down, no more to roam. They had adopted me! Soon it was shearing time, but there was no consolation for us in that, for there wasn't a whole fleece of wool between the four of them.

Early that spring Angus decided to let the summer grazing on his big pasture again. It seemed to make sense because most of his sheep would be receiving free board and lodging all over the valley, I thought,rather bitterly.Some of the regular habitués of grass lettings had been heard expressing doubts that, in fact, Angus had actually applied the two hundredweights of fertilizer per acre which had been promised at his grass letting two years ago. This would have considerably enhanced the value of the grazing. And last year, they reckoned, he had simply driven his tractor up and down the field, just before the night of the letting so that the wheel-marks thus made in the grass, still visible, would give the impression that the fertilizer spreading job had actually been done.

Angus Mackay however, was nothing if not resourceful, so before the night of the grass-letting he arranged that a trailer loaded with a bit more than a ton of fertilizer (about a hundred and eighty pound's worth) was parked conveniently near the field entrance. The bags were labelled"20-10-10",(i.e.20% nitrogen, 10% phosphate,and 10% potash). That would be bound to allay any suspicions!

The auctioneer announced the terms of letting; "From the day of letting to the end of September!" he said, and started searching the assembled company for bids."Oh,yes, Gentlemen!"he interrupted himself," Mr MacKay says that he will be spreading that trailer load of 'twenty-ten-ten' on the field during the next day or two. "What am I bid?" And the bidding started in earnest, moving swiftly to a close in only seconds, not minutes. Bidding had started at the somewhat laughable figure of "fifty pounds", from some optimist. Norman ignored that, and immediately said, "Thank you, Sir! Two hundred and fifty pounds!" Five more bids brought it to its final figure."That's it, Gentlemen! Let to Mounsey of the Brigg! Three hundred and ninety pounds!"

Mr Mounsey took his pipe out of his mouth and said, laconically to Angus "I'll send one of my lads down with a tractor in the morning to spread that fertilizer!" For once Angus was speechless.

By July Angus's eight lambs were fit for market. Of course they were three-quarter-bred Suffolks;'bred for early maturity'. Old Frank urged me to keep the two best lambs, and take the rest back to Angus. And on reflection it would have been about the right remuneration for keeping his animals for almost a year, while in the meantime he had been letting his own grassland as surplus to requirements. But I hesitated.

One day early in July, Fred and I returned from a fencing job to find that Angus had paid us a visit and picked up his Swaledale ewes and their lambs. He probably guessed that the lambs could go to market right away. I was furious. Not even a vote of thanks! We coupled-up the small trailer to the tractor and went round to Sycamore Farm at top speed. I was really steamed up.

"You've picked up your sheep then, Angus." I said, as evenly as I could manage. "Yes,thanks". That was it I thought! "Thanks"! "Angus,"I said sternly, "I'm going to give you three alternatives!" "Alternatives! What do you mean;"alternatives"? he asked mildly. I was absolutely seething. "Well, you can go and get one of those lambs and put it in this trailer, as payment for nearly a years keep!" "Should be two lambs at least!" muttered Fred, audibly. "Or" I said "you can go in the house and bring me out a cheque for twenty pounds!" "Thirty pounds,more like!" interjected Fred. Again I ignored him *I* was the one who was handling this! "What's the third 'alternative'?" said Angus,faintly curious."I'll have you charged with sheep stealing!" I said angrily.

McKay walked into the house shaking his head and muttering,but finally emerged with a cheque in his hand. I stuffed it in my pocket and we returned home in triumph. We both savoured the moment of victory as I took out the crumpled cheque and opened it out flat. With a sudden thought I looked at the date. "Aha,it's not post-dated!" I said with relief, handing it over to Fred.He carefully examined the cheque and then handed it back. "No," he said, "but it's only made out for nineteen pun ten!"

Chapter 4

The Curious Case of the Curling Carpet

Alderman William Potter, County Councillor, was quite a sober chap. He more or less had to be, for he was from a long line of Methodists and public servants. William farmed the 'Old Parks', a farm of between four and five hundred acres lying between Kirkoswald and Glassonby and overlooking a small tributary of the River Eden. Although the small trout stream's name is 'Dale Raven' it is always referred to as the 'Dale Raffen'. A hard - working man, William called an evenings fishing there, his only 'vice'.

William Potter and later his sons Alan and Joe - all three of them local preachers - were hosts to influential personalities of the Methodist Church as well as from local government. One of their eminent Methodist visitors on many occasions was Gipsy Smith, the stocky little full-blooded Gipsy evangelist who could fill any venue in the land with the power of his oratory, much as his American counterpart Billy Graham has done in recent years. Later on his nephew the Reverend G. Bramwell Evans who was the Methodist minister at the Central Hall at Carlisle, almost became, through his frequent visits, one of the Potter family. And my sister Margaret did just that when she married Alan, and Bramwell was the officiating minister.

Few people can now remember "Childrens Hour" on 'steam radio', whose listeners had the world of nature brought vividly to life by Romany's unique vibrant voice.With his dark lean aquiline face he would have been a natural television personality today. His books,"*Romany and Raq*","*Wanderings with Romany*" and many others are still treasured. Romany's ashes are actually buried on the Parks. Fifty years after his death a large company gathered for a commemoration service by the little memorial where his ashes were scattered. This was the culmination of a week-long series of commemorative programmes on Radio Cumbria.

I remember taking Bramwell to photograph a buzzard's nest on a cliffside of the Loogill ravine on Hartside when I was quite a small boy. This was ages before zoom lenses became commoplace. He just had to get much nearer. So Romany had scaled the cliff edge in his bare feet, with his prehensile toes gripping every protruding rock. He admitted that this practice of having to put his bare feet in the "gunge", wasn't particularly pleasant when he had climbed guana-covered rocks when taking shots of sea birds nesting on Ailsa Craig. But he said that nevertheless, he felt much safer barefoot.

He built his hide some distance from the nest and moved it a little closer every day until he was reasonably satisfied with the prospects of success. On the final day he sent me back to his car parked on the road a mile or so away and simply told me to wait. His theory was that birds can't count and that the circling buzzards would assume that he, too, had left the vicinity!

The name the 'Old Parks' is thought to indicate that it was once part of the medieval hunting ground of Inglewood Forest, which once covered a huge tract of land in the centre of Cumberland and the original function of the farmhouse would have been as a hunting lodge for the nobility and the favoured who participated in the chase. Red sandstone from Lazonby Fell was used for walls staircase and floors and, like thousands more the house had no damp-course and would have been quite damp. In any case the kitchen would have its stone-flags scrubbed at least once a week. The front parlour was the venue for learned discussions on the topics of the day. Now the Old Parks is a large beef and sheep farm, with all the expensive machinery and buildings which enable two people to feed and handle its large flock of sheep,and the herd of beef cattle. But in William's day there would have been at least five or six men, some of whom lived-in, and at least one dairymaid. This was for less than a quarter of present day stocking levels.

But the opportunities to sell produce off the farm were increasing, and about forty gallons of milk were carted daily to Lazonby station, about three miles away, en route for a cheese factory. Every morning one of the three horsemen would yoke-up a cart and take the seventeen-gallon milk cans to the station. These cans weighed nearly two hundredweights when they were full, and were wider at the base than at the top and this slightly conical shape made the task of rolling them along a station platform while still almost upright - by someone with practice - so much easier. But it needed two strong men to heave them up into a cart.

The dairying enterprise was started long before such refinements as refrigerated tanks, or even milk coolers were thought of; so under the assumption that the milk would cool much faster the can lids were left off the evening's milking, "to let the steam out". By morning there would be several inches of cream at the narrow top of the can.

One morning the second horsemen was "yoking-up", and the heavy cans were about to be loaded on the cart when the lad who was banging the lid on the last of the cans,shouted "Hey! There's a dead cat in this one!" He gingerly fished out the very dead animal and prepared to fling it on the midden.(Everything was really organic in those days) But as he started to swing the unfortunate cat the dairy girl screamed "Stop! Stop! Scrape the cream off!"

Young Alan was the one who looked after the pigs. There were only three sows, but with two litters a year - each - it meant that there were hardly ever less than sixteen or even twenty most recently weaned piglets. These were Alan's responsibility and he happened to be crossing the yard one morning to see to them, when he witnessed the minor disaster.

Joseph, his elder brother and the strong lad recently hired, were loading the heavy cans of milk into the cart which was bound for the station, when it happened. The last of the tall cans didn't quite achieve perpendicularity as it was heaved up onto the cart. Later analysis was that "the horse had kicked out at a passing collie, the cart had moved slightly and so had totally destabilised the can just at the critical moment". The tall can shot towards them, and fell to the ground, fortunately doing them no injury. As the can hit the ground,however, the lid flew off and seventeen gallons of milk shot over the yard.

As they stood aghast at this calamity, Alan's presence of mind offered a partial solution."Let those young pigs out!" he shouted. The farm lad lifted the latch of the pig-sty, and the squealing pigs - scenting the milk - needed no encouragement to dash over to the white foaming pools, and eagerly drink what they could before the last of it soaked into the cobbled yard.

A year or two later the Potter family became aware of something rather strange and possibly a little sinister. When they retired for the night there was an orderly candlelit procession up the stone stairs. They would have had a quiet evening in the dim light of a paraffin lamp. Possibly Hannah or Charlotte may have played a few hymns on the piano before bedtime. But when all was quiet and settled for the night there was, in fact, something rather odd going on in the parlour. It took quite a long time for the family to become aware of it for the parlour wasn't in daily use. Sometimes it might be weeks before the arrival of some important personage caused the front fire to be lit.

It took quite a while before the family had all compared notes. They concluded that something inexplicable was undoubtedly happening. It was deeply upsetting especially for the womenfolk. One by one they had all eventually noticed that a corner of the carpet (the only one in the house) was often turned over in a sort of double fold. For many weeks someone simply turned it back flat. But the first person in the room next morning found it once more turned in its peculiar double fold. Other simple remedies were tried. The carpet was turned bodily around, which was in fact quite a feat, for of course all the heavy old fashioned furniture had to be moved about. But no matter, the next morning, the carpet in that corner was turned and folded back as before. They all agreed that it was very odd.

William resolved to sit up all night and find out when the carpet actually turned. So one winter's night when the fire had been lit during the day, and therefore to some extent the room had been aired he commenced his lonely vigil. He was a frugal man, more so than most, in an era which was and had to be, very frugal. It simply would not occur to him to keep the fire going all night, by putting on a few logs. But he was prepared to light a candle when he could no longer see across the room. He could hear the ticking of the grandfather clock in the hall, and for a moment he remembered that that was where he kept his shotgun. He toyed briefly with the idea of perhaps having it a bit closer to hand. Although he was listening intently, he knew that neither floors or staircase, both of which were solid sandstone, could possibly creak,and the sounds outside were farm sounds with which he had been familiar all his life.

"Anyway", he told himself sternly, "a carpet doesn't turn itself over, on its own!"He wasn't a superstitious man."Methodists simply don't believe in that rubbish,and that's that", he thought. He began to wonder if it had all been caused by a playful cat which had mistakenly been left indoors. Suddenly a cold draught swept round the room and his hair stood on end. The candle gave a splutter and went out. Like most farmers he was a practical sort of man and decided on a course of action. He cautiously felt his way to the door and in a very thoughtful mood felt his way up the stairs and went to bed.

His wife hadn't slept well for weeks. The whole mysterious happenings had had a very unsettling effect on her. They preyed on her mind to an almost unbearable degree and "Something had to be done". Eventually William was persuaded to call the estate workmen who without ceremony lifted the corner flagstones and dug down several feet. Then they found an almost complete human skeleton. It was later assumed to be from the middle-ages. There was a shred of cloth - some said that they thought it was or had been red. And a few brass buttons gave credence to the theory that the remains were those of a huntsman who had clearly come to an untimely and violent end. The bones were removed and reverently re-interred elsewhere. The carpet never turned again.

Chapter 5

Egg on My Face

After a somewhat tortuous trip by train from Newcastle-upon-Tyne, and round the now defunct railway following the glorious coastal route round south west Scotland to the boat at Stranraer, we had found ourselves in Northern Ireland. The Regiment had left all its guns and equipment to whoever succeeded us in County Durham and likewise we were to take-over, lock stock and barrel, at Loughbrickland. A veritable Quartermaster's nightmare.

There was a tragedy that first night. Most of the lads had left our camp which was largely located within the precincts of a small mansion at the little village and gone off to the neighbouring small market town of Banbridge - under the assumption that the one hostelry in the village, the 'Seven Stars' pub would be full to overflowing - to try out the local beer or maybe porter, the somewhat cheaper version of stout. A sort of Regimental reconnaissance.

One of the lads searching in the black-out for a convenient field to use as a convenience, put his hand on a low wall and vaulted over into what he obviously thought was an open field, and fell twenty five feet to his death. Daylight, or well-lit streets would have shown that he had been at the top of what would now be known as a 'flyover', where the gradient of the steep street had been eased a little by making a steep cutting for the main road traffic. The nearest field was half a mile away.

The camp at Loughbrickland consisted of a large number of Nissen huts sited around the periphery of the grounds of a quite modest mansion,which naturally had been bagged as officer's quarters. We rankers were in the Nissen huts. There were usually twelve or maybe fourteen to a hut. In the middle of each hut was a small stove. To have one's bunk near the stove was a mixed blessing because naturally - as there was nowhere else to sit - these bunks became the obvious seats for everyone. One can't have it all ways!

One night as we sat around the stove I fried a slice of lovely home-cured Cumberland ham which my mother had included in her parcels for my birthday. I had had to remove the 'lid' of the stove to get enough heat to fry the thick ham in a biscuit-tin lid. The smell was driving all the lads green with envy. For the *piéce de resistance* I also fried a duck egg which had been given to me by a local farmer. My culinary efforts were the object of ribald, though envious comment, but I was quite prepared to eat my meal with all the others enviously looking on and drooling like the old advert of the 'Bisto Kids'. I might have been able to cut the slice of ham into twelve, but there was no way I could do it with the egg.

The ham was ready and waiting on my plate, filling the place with its tantalising aroma as I fried the egg in my biscuit-tin lid. Naturally there was no 'egg-slice' and when the egg was ready for turning I was in some difficulty. The problem was about to be solved by tossing the egg like a pancake, but unfortunately at the critical moment it dropped like a stone right through the hole in the stove-top and vanished in the glowing coals. There was a prolonged burst of laughter from the envious onlookers and the egg instantly became a part of regimental history. Decades later, at annual regimental re-unions, someone would be sure to raise a laugh by saying "Hey,Kidd! Do you remember that egg you fried at Loughbrickland?" Not many eggs thus achieve a sort of immortality.

Until 4pm there wasn't supposed to be any comfort in the huts. To be honest there wasn't a lot *after* that time either. Of course we could prepare the stove for lighting but until that time our kit had to retain its formal regimented state and thus there was nowhere to sit. All ex soldiers will recall the particular pattern which was favoured by their unit.There were small differences but the main feature of the arrangement was the carefully folded regulation three blankets two of which formed the core,as it were, while the other blanket was folded round. Then the spare pair of boots, inverted to show the Orderly Officer on his inspection, firstly that they were in good repair and secondly that they displayed the standard thirteen studs which someone had said was the optimum number. Then one's mess tin and other bits and pieces in the authorized pattern completed the kit.

I was in some difficulty with my blankets because I jealously owned a contraband fourth blanket, and also a sheet. (absolute decadence!) This had obviously stuck in Jimmy's mind for over fifty years, for last Christmas he said quite accusingly "You had a *sheet*!" The sheet and extra blanket were concealed both from my hut-mates and the Orderly Officer's close inspection by extremely careful folding. Other contraband could be concealed in vehicles.

The Orderly Officer's duties included visiting the serving of main meals to ask if there were any complaints. This was apparently laid down somewhere in King's Regulations. One day as I was the man who happened to be at the end of the table, I was urged to complain about something or other, it was overcooked, undercooked, or just insufficient. One forgets. So I stood up. "Yes, Kidd?" asked the somewhat supercilious young subaltern. By this time they seemed to be getting younger. I said my piece. The young lieutenant turned to the others and asked how they found their servings. As one man they all averred that theirs was excellent. I sat down deflated but vowing never to be a spokesman again.

But coal, lack of, was a problem. Pilfering of extra coal went on until Regimental Orders one day stated, "Pilfering of coal will not be tolerated". This was to be strictly enforced. The R.S.M. got a working party to erect a high barbed-wire barricade round the large coal heap. There would be a locked barbed-wire 'door',to prevent pilferers. We of the working party had naturally included in the structure a secret entrance, for our own nocturnal purposes. But the R.S.M. had also arranged for the whole heap to be sprayed by a stirrup-pump with a good thick coat of whitewash. This might have been an extension of the old Forces adage "If it moves, salute it! If it doesn't, whitewash it!"

The R.S.M's ingenious idea forced us to acquire our own private whitewash supply so that we could conceal the incriminating evidence of our nightly depredations. But whitewash, coal,and barbed-wire are somewhat incompatible commodities and it was considered quite a feat that the 'pilfering' remained undetected.

Young Dunk and I sneaked away from our bivouacs while we were on a week-end manoeuvre on the slopes of the Mourne Mountains, for we had heard distant sounds of a ceilidh starting up in a church hall. We entered the building optimistically to some Irish jig, which we felt would be a bit on the fast side for our heavy boots. Immediately on our entry, however, the music stoppped, and we were the target of all eyes. There was a sort of consultation and a young girl was pushed up onto the stage where she sang a mournful ballad. Something after this style; "My son, my son, was shot in old Dublin; he died in the cause of old Ireland". All eyes were on us. Unfriendly eyes were a bit of a shock to us and we realised that prospects weren't at all good, and so retreated with as much dignity as we could muster.

It seems incredible that there had been not the slightest advance warning from the Army, of the ideological divide, in this lovely country. Notwithstanding that, our regiment had to deliver a number of now redundant French Seventy-fives - that wonderful old gun from the first world war - to the army of Southern Ireland. It was another of the puzzles. We began to wonder where they would be aiming!

In due course there was leave back to England. This was a prolonged process involving nearly two days travel by sea and rail with, of course a travel-warrant. But there was a civilian air service to Glasgow from Belfast, costing just over £5, which put it quite out of reach of a private soldier at fourteen shillings a week (seventy pence!) even if about half of it wasn't with-held to help finance a marriage allowance.

But my Grandfather Watson had left each of his sixteen grandsons the sum of a hundred pounds. 'To be paid when they attained the age of twenty one'. As I was quite small when Grandfather died my portion had increased with interest over the years to over a hundred and sixty pounds. I would possibly be one of less than half a dozen rankers in the regiment with a bank account. I'm sure that Grandfather would have been delighted to see how much of his money I was spending with the Salvation Army; in their "Red- Shield" Canteens.

Grandfather had once been attending a neighbour's farm sale. It was tradition that one had to get one's 'name in the book' at a neighbour's sale. And 'neighbour' included virtually anyone within a six mile radius. Following this old tradition was difficult if one was already retired, but Grandfather bought half a dozen kitchen chairs and arrived back to his home in Kirkoswald with the chairs on a horse drawn cart and informed Granny of the bargain purchase. She was a placid woman and wasn't normally of a scolding disposition, but this time she unburdened herself of her comprehensive view of the chairs. She mentioned that they had been married nearly forty years. They had enough chairs for the whole of the village to sit on. In short they didn't want any more even if they were for nothing and she wasn't going to have more chairs in the house! Grandfather mumbled something about "taking them over to Jenny", in other words, my fairly recently married mother. She would be more than pleased with them, he said. "Oh" said Grandmother," If you're going over to Jenny's, will you take her a note?" The said note was hurriedly written, and Grandfather - instead of unloading the furniture from the cart - found himself setting off the two extra miles to Lazonby. On arrival he handed over the note to my mother. It read; "Dear Jenny, on no account have these chairs in the house!"

But forty years later, in Northern Ireland, with some of Grandfather's legacy I was in the extremely fortunate position of being able to afford a return ticket on the little airline to Glasgow. I could then get the southbound train and travel the rest of the way on my travel-warrant and be home by coffee time the same morning. To do the same journey by sea and train would have taken two days, in each direction!

The plane was a tiny two-engined cabin biplane with seats for seven passengers, and it was a relief that the data which one could see on the 'dashboard' over the pilot's shoulder included the reassuring information that while the maximum speed on both engines was said to be one hundred and thirty miles an hour, one engine alone would enable the plane to fly at ninety five miles an hour. It didn't say if this claim had ever been substantiated. But I was back home by coffee time!

Chapter 6

The Great Attic Clear-out

The men were coming to insulate the attic and one thing led to another, as it always does. It seemed an opportune time to have a good clear-out of all sorts of rubbish which had gradually accumulated since the farm had been bought in 1920. That there would have to be changes after Father's death went without saying. Mother was a practical woman who would have made a good pioneer blazing a westward trail to California. She made up her mind and said, "Get rid of it all,find a safe spot and burn it. Burn it all! Otherwise we will *never* get rid of it". So she went off for the week-end and left the task to me. There was the old school photograph about four feet long with the traditional double photo of some daredevil who had dared the wrath of the Headmaster by running round the back of the group from one end to the other end, while the photographer rotated his camera.

Why all this junk had ever been put up there was a mystery. There seemed to be dozens of leather-bound photograph albums, bursting at the seams with studio portraits of heavily bearded Victorian gentlemen. And ladies with their hugely impressive hats which made me think of Carmen Miranda,with her extrovert turbans covered with fruit. They had all felt certain that posterity would see these splendid photographs.

Each portrait would have entailed a day-trip to a Carlisle studio. What a pity that after all this expense and travelling, none of them had thought to insert their names and dates on the back. It was sad but they would all have to go. But I would have to keep that huge map of Canada; it seemed far too good to burn. And the amazing photograph of the entire village population gathered in front of our Parish Church. Probably taken in 1890, it was undoubtedly part of the village celebrations of Queen Victoria's golden jubilee.

Father had been the youngest of five children, all born in a thatched cottage at Glassonby where the family name is found on the Parish Church records of the Church of St Michael as far back as 1600. All records prior to that date are reputed to have been destroyed in a fire. They had all been yeoman-farmers. That is to say they owned enough land to support themselves, albeit at the usual low standards of the day, but owed no allegiance to any local squire.

Strict discipline was the order of the day, and like all their neighbours they were virtually self-sufficient. Two or three pigs a year would be killed to provide some pork and more bacon - albeit so fat that few people could stomach it nowadays. 'Streaky-bacon', right up to World War Two, meant at most one miserable streak of lean in a whole rasher of salty fat. 'Brockshire' was more palatable, being the salted carcase of a sheep. Some of which might be eaten fried, roasted or boiled. Boiled mutton! What a sobering thought. And with the odd miscellaneous bits in 'tatie-pots', and the hams and sides salted away for the lean winter days to come.

There was a small acreage of oats, just enough for the little farm's various livestock, as well as providing the household's porridge. The water mill was only half a mile away. Hay and oat straw provided the winter fodder for the few cattle and enough butter was made for family use. A small acreage of swedes was grown to ensure that there was enough succulent winter feed for the stock. Most families would be able to eat a rabbit or two from time to time. Self sufficiency was the main ambition.

From time to time however there would have been diversions. The trip to Penrith market on a Tuesday would take about an hour in the trap,and allow the sale of surplus butter, eggs, and the occasional chicken.The journey home would bring essentials like salt and sugar, flour, candles and paraffin. Clogs lasted for years, subject, of course, to an occasional complete renewal of the iron 'caukers'. Inexcusable failure to do so would mean rapid wearing-

out of the wooden soles within a week. There were no luxuries for anyone, and daily newspapers were confined to the towns. All the children had attended Addingham School under the headmaster's stern tutelage. When part of the school playground needed cobbles he had sent the children to a quarry several hundred yards away each 'playtime' with the injunction to each pupil to 'bring back a cobble' for the playground. In time the work had been completed without any drain on the meagre funds available.

Dry-closets were still the norm - some of them two-seaters - and although piped water was just round the corner, so to speak, buckets of water still had to be carried from the well. Toilet paper hadn't even been invented. Right up to the outbreak of World War Two, in 1939, my Aunt Ada at Lancaster still maintained that pages from J.D.William's catalogue were 'just as good'.

Sunday was the day of rest and was strictly observed, with the two services at Church or Chapel and Sunday School in the afternoons. On the Sabbath day there was the absolute minimum of essential farm work undertaken. The morning and evening services were the main social events and several relatives would be 'local preachers'. 'Temperance' was an aim supported by those who looked on the Annual 'Demonstrations' of 'Bands of Hope' and 'Sons of Temperance' as the highlights of the year. The latter organisation was usually refered to - somewhat inaccurately - as t'Sunday Temperance'! The Demonstration was always at Appleby. (Why Appleby? Was it a hotbed of drunkeness?). The little town would be crowded with brass-bands, and silver bands, and banner-carrying delegations from most villages.

'News' was mainly confined to that of local interest, and national and international news took several days or even weeks to percolate. The South African War was at its height, and Mafeking was besieged by the Boer forces. For news of these events the railway, which thirty five odd years earlier had pierced the Eden valley with a scenic line from Leeds to Carlisle, was the main source of reliable national news.

The nearest station was then Little Salkeld and it was from thence that the announcement came of the relief of Mafeking and the postman who had brought the good news to Glassonby was challenged as to the veracity of his statement. "Well", he had said firmly, "T'rumour's ga-en strang at La-al Saffeld!" The report was then considered to be unchallengeable.

My father had, some years earlier, been to Manchester. The news of his departure shook his contemporaries at Glassonby, but it turned out that he had gone to an aunt there, of whose existence he had never heard. With her husband, it seemed, she ran a shop in Ardwick Green, and they were looking for a family member who could step into their shoes when they would be shortly retiring. Father was despatched on this momentous journey. He was never to be so far 'south' again and hugely enjoyed the hurly-burly of Manchester. It was a completely new world to him and he reported back of the glowing prospects awaiting. Unfortunately in his last weekly letter home he had innocently reported that Aunt Dora and Uncle Jim's enterprise included a prosperous section of the shop called - he thought - an 'Off-licence'. By return of post he got instructions from his horrified mother to "come home at once!" Thus the road to perdition was narrowly avoided.

There was a more favourable outcome however with one of the shop's regular customers. He had a large butcher's business in both Manchester and Leeds and from a casual conversation it emerged that the population of these cities had an insatiable but unfulfilled desire for rabbit meat. Father promised to see if he could investigate the prospects of daily deliveries by train to Leeds.

The resulting business relationship, mutually lucrative, was to last over twenty-five years, although the two parties never again met. Father was sent a trial consignment of a couple of wicker rabbit-crates. All he had to do was to send back the crates by rail to Leeds each night on the evening train, loaded with a dozen 'couples'. The rabbits had to be 'coupled' together neatly by the simple means of pushing a rear leg through a small incision in front of the rabbits opposite 'hamstring', and the legs of the second half of the 'couple were threaded through those of the first so that they could hang in pairs over two stout sticks which were an integral part of the wicker-work crates. In this way the suspended rabbit carcases were given the optimum amount of air circulating round them.

A photograph, circa 1895, shows Father - a young man in clogs - setting off on this career and taking some of the first crates to Lazonby station; with his hard working mother - who had been left a widow at an early age - watching admiringly with my Aunt Maggie. Even in clogs Father wore a tie. I never saw him without one.

By this time the thatched cottage had been demolished and replaced with a substantial stone dwelling every stone of which had been transported from the quarry to the local builder by Father with a horse and cart.

There was an absolutely insatiable demand for rabbits, according to the Manchester butcher; "Just send me as many as you can get hold of." Father endeavoured to fill this vacuum by enlisting large numbers of professional rabbit-catchers, gamekeepers, farmers and even poachers who simply turned up at Lazonby station in sufficient time to have their consignments recorded by an off-duty porter, before they were loaded on the evening train to Leeds. There was therefore no need to even have any premises. Empty crates for the next day's consignment would have already arrived on the 'down-train'. Father arrived at the station every Saturday morning and settled all the accounts before setting off to Penrith to bank his cheque for the previous week's deliveries.

Around this time there was romance. Father had met my mother at Kirkoswald Chapel Anniversary and subsequently fulfilled the almost statutory obligation of attending Sunday chapel there with her for several months before proposing marriage. A three-mile walk there and three back, obviously made his intentions clear and they were married in 1912 in the chapel Grandfather Watson had built a decade earlier.

Before my father left Glassonby he had been almost persuaded to emigrate to Canada. One of his contemporaries had returned after only a few years with glowing tales of the money which could be made there. Those who for family reasons couldn't follow the advice to emigrate were given the chance to invest. Few had funds to spare but Father gave his schoolfellow £250 for investment as he thought best. There was no formal agreement, for they were old friends. Within a year the astounding 'interest' of £50 was reported, and my father willingly agreed to the suggestion that it should 'stand-on' for further investment. One or two more insiders were allowed to participate on similar terms. It seemed almost too good to be true. The trap was set.

Then Father was offered the opportunity of a lifetime. There was a section of land, a square mile, available just outside Portage La Prairie, an up-and-coming town in Manitoba. His old friend now had become a partner in an established real-estate company. He thought my father would be interested in the firm's map of Canada which showed "Land owned or controlled by Metcalfe and Burley, shown in red". This was the enormous map from the attic which had so nearly been destroyed. A brief study showed red sections in every Province south of the Arctic Circle.The man was obviously doing very well indeed.

Metcalfe offered Father this section of land for £9,000. It was a 'snip' at this price, as unknown to the average investor, he said, a railway was about to be constructed which would pass through the very edge of the said section and enhance the prospects even further. The opportunities were momentous, but time was of the essence. Up to now Metcalf hadn't offered it elsewhere. He had thought of my father first. Father much appreciated being thought of in this way.

He was a naturally cautious man and nine thousand pounds was a lot of money at the time. It would have bought a whole street of terrace houses in Carlisle. But Metcalfe made it easier for him.He could buy the section by instalments. His old friend would be sent up to two thousand a year until it was paid for. The suggestion was accepted and the deal was closed on that basis. Sadly there would have to be interest payments on the balance outstanding but he appreciated that business is business.

With the forthcoming marriage in mind Father had bought 'South View' at Lazonby where all the offspring were born, with the exception of Theodosia, who was born a few years after we had moved up the road to Rose Bank Farmhouse, now North Bank.

The rabbit business was growing steadily bigger and proving very lucrative indeed. He must have cleared millions of rabbits from the Eden Valley. Would that someone would do the same today when wild rabbits are seen in domestic gardens and even the village churchyards. So he was enabled to buy the farm. It never made a fortune, however, for times in farming were getting steadily worse. He actually retired from farming and let the farm, for by this time he had decided to trade in both cattle and sheep and with Tom Harrison he bought literally hundreds of thousands of lambs each autumn from as far north as Dingwall and Oban. After a year the farm's tenant had had the offer of a farm which was twice as big but at half the rent, an offer which he would have been a fool to refuse. So Father had to start actively farming again, a year after he had retired. In the meantime he employed a manager for the rabbit business, and eventually gave him the business. Seven or eight years later the business had been 'managed' to extinction.

In addition to the farming, Father did what he felt was more interesting than selling mere rabbits. He bought and sold hundreds of sheep and cattle locally. He had an unofficial sort of partnership with Tom Harrison and between them they bought - over the years - huge numbers of Scottish lambs. These arrived in trainloads at Lazonby station the next day where customers and drovers were waiting to drive them the few miles to their ultimate destinations. The railway company so valued their trade that Tom and my father only had to ask, to have an express train stopped at the small station for their convenience!

Tom was a splendid traveller and could sleep anywhere and eat whatever was put in front of him. In fact he invariably ordered for three, and when the waitress looked round enquiringly he simply murmured "Oh, he'll be here in a minute!" and then finish the extra serving himself. On one occasion when they were going up to Scotland together Tom curled up in a corner and went to sleep almost immediately, as was his wont, with his overcoat completely covering his head. As they approached Carstairs -

which happened to have what was then referred to, in the inaccurate fashion of the time, as an 'asylum', (now its a modern prison) - the ticket collector examined Dad's ticket and then looked enquiringly towards Tom. Father had a mischievous streak and said, ever so quietly, "Carstairs!" The ticket collector silently left the compartment endeavouring to close the door as quietly as possible.

By 1920 Father had paid off the Portage La Prairie property but now with a growing family he felt that perhaps this was a speculation he shouldn't have made in the first place, so he instructed Metcalfe to sell it. I had to try and deduce the contents of Father's letters, from the wording of the replies for he didn't keep a copy of his own letters - although Metcalfe's replies are carefully filed. Father was advised to wait, as the market was going through a temporary blip.'Perhaps in a couple of years...who knows?'.

Going through the later letters in the file they show - over a period of several years - an increasing anxiety on Father's part, and a growing suspicion that all was not right. Metcalfe was advising him to hang-on and all would be well. Father finally must have insisted that the land be sold for the best price obtainable, but Metcalfe's last filed letter stated that times were now even worse, there was no chance of selling at any price and that he personally, had had to get the best job that he could get, albeit at a paltry wage "simply to keep the wolf from the door". At this stage Father had evidently decided to abandon further attempts to recover his money. Like other serious business misfortunes, he never mentioned it again.

Father died in 1946 and incidentally for some - to me - unfathomable reason virtually cut me from his will. Maybe he had thought I wouldn't return from the war. Mother was outraged at the revelation but couldn't do anything to rectify it.

She was an indomitable woman. Apart from bringing up six children, and keeping nearly five hundred hens, there were many other interests. She somehow persuaded Father that it would be a highly desirable thing to have a tennis lawn. So old Jim Pool who was a ditcher by trade, was employed to level the sloping site using only barrow, spade, and a spirit level,and sow it down to grass and also build an open fronted shelter which Mother always called her 'pavilion'. Jim completed the work within a month.

Mother entertained, she organised a ladies choir which won awards at Carlisle Music Festival, she was a leading spirit in village events designed to pay off the debt for our magnificent Village Hall, and even painted the scenery for the operettas. She also played the 'cello forming a family trio with Nancy on the piano and Archie on the violin. Several of her oil paintings, done as a teenage girl, survive.

Archie, destined to be one of the leading engineers of his generation with a lifetime total of over four hundred patents, had at the age of eleven, during one of his school holidays fixed up an old motor-bike engine on a wooden mounting in an unused pig-sty to generate electricity in the house, long before what was known as the Grid-Scheme was initiated. He had arranged matters so that when the last light was switched off the motor-bike engine stopped. He also made the first 'wireless' set in the village and rigged up a loud-speaker for one of Mother's little 'garden-parties'. They could hear the music at Scale Hill, half a mile away. It was a sensation.

Mother agreed, a shade reluctantly, to my offer to try and salvage something from the Canadian fiasco. I wrote to the Canadian Land Titles office in Manitoba and asked about the present situation regarding my father's land. It was quite exciting to speculate as to the possibilities. Maybe my mother would be the owner of vast swathes of land, now possibly within the city of Portage la Prairie itself.

In due course there was a reply. It tersely stated that "the Section of land referred to is Crown Land in the name of the Province of Manitoba, and has never; at any time, been in the name of your father or the real estate company Metcalfe and Burley."

I wrote a letter to Metcalfe in a last-ditch attempt to salvage something from the debacle. I threatened that unless an acceptable offer of restitution was made to my mother there would be no alternative to instituting criminal charges. Several months later my letter returned, evidently having drawn a blank at eight or nine different locations in Canada. Someone had written on the envelope in pencil; "Thomas Henry Metcalfe died in Toronto about nine years ago".

Chapter 7

The "Lights of London"

The Village Hall had been the venue for functions for several generations and was starting to look its age and becoming a shade too small for the increasing population of the twenties. One of the village worthies (aptly named Mr Hall, in fact) resolved to do something about it. Why he bore the Christian name of Hindson is sadly unknown nowadays, although, in fact, several parts of the village bear that name.

Strangely enough there is a portait of the distinguished looking man himself in the Jubilee Room of the Village Hall, although the committee hasn't got round, so far, to affixing his name thereto. Still, as my late brother Harold used to say,"There's many a hundred years not broken into yet". And it took over fifty years to have the name of the building itself attached.

This splendid additional building was actually started in the twenties before the 'Grid-Scheme' brought electricity to the village, and as there was an ample supply of free water flowing in pipes down from the slopes of the Pennines, it was decided in the interim to light the Hall with electricity generated by a 'Pelton-wheel'. In essence it was a miniature mill-wheel enclosed in a sort of casing and onto which a fierce jet of water was directed. The waste water, denuded of its energy, was then allowed to flow into the nearby beck.

Most of the population was pressed into fund-raising activities to pay off the debt to the local auction company, which had, most generously, provided an interest-free loan which, in fact, was paid off in only a few years. One money-raising event was a gift-sale and I was instructed by my father to donate my pair of Guinea Pigs. Even at that tender age I could never understand why they were called "pigs" when every boy knew that they were most certainly rodents, and knew that they originated in the Andes which are some considerable distance from Guinea, either Old or New. Father was, for some obscure reason, fed-up with my cavies and was determined to take this glorious opportunity to get rid of them.

There were all sorts of gifts. Both livestock and dead-stock. Even a sheep! There was a pen of hens which someone said 'were only old boilers', potatoes, turnips, apples and a load of manure, which fortunately was to be delivered direct to the purchaser's allotment. This actually was a useful gift as most villagers in the twenties depended on their allotments for all their vegetable needs. There were also loads of logs 'to be delivered', odd bits of furniture, even a wireless set, a bicycle (with a flat tyre). and many many more items than I can remember. And of course, the cavies.

The professional services of Stanley, from the distant auctioneer branch of the family, had been enlisted to sell all the items. When he eventually came to my contribution I was pleased that he described them correctly. "What am I bid for this beautiful pair of cavies?" Father leaned over to tell him that my rather handsome cage, with bars made from old bike-spokes, was included in the sale. "Yes,the whole outfit is included. An absolute bargain for someone! What am I bid?" asked Stanley, looking round the assembly for customers.

Sadly he had to report to my father,who was hovering nearby, that there was not a single starting bid."What were his instructions?" Father and he went into a huddle, and Stanley emerged to announce that 'the Guinea-pigs, sorry, Cavies, would be given to the first boy who put up his hand'. At this amazing offer a hand went up. Then it wobbled and seemed about to go down. Father intervened rapidly and said "Get them passed-down, Stanley, before he cocks on the deal!"

The next big event which I remember was a show called "The Lights of London", brought "at enormous expense" from the capital. There were several performers who 'doubled' in various acts, but the one which made a lasting impression was one,

Martin Breedis! He was billed as the 'strongest man in the world'. He was certainly very very strong. He could drive a six-inch nail - through a two inch plank supplied by Horatio Smith, the joiner who had recently completed the building work itself; *with the palm of his hand!* And there seemed no doubt that the nail and the plank were genuine.

Then he lay prone on the stage and had the piano lifted by four sturdy members of the audience, onto a square board on his chest as he lay on the platform. As soon as he was 'comfortable' with this burden, the musician would add a piano-stool, and then go through a lively repertoire!

For the *piéce de resistance* Martin offered to lift the six heaviest men in the audience. The two heaviest men in the village who were at the performance were Horatio Smith, himself, and Joe Paley, the butcher, both of whom would probably be over sixteen stones, whereas I - a mere stripling of maybe eight or nine stones, was the lightest and made-up the required number.

Breedis lay on his back again, but this time balanced a heavy twelve-foot plank on his feet. Then he invited the two heaviest volunteers to place themselves leaning over the plank, followed in turn by the rest of the volunteers. Breedis gave a tentative lift, followed by a small adjustment of his feet to equalize the weight, whereupon he actually lifted the six of us several times clear of the floor with his powerful legs and moved us gently up and down for several seconds.

Years later, we heard that Breedis had met an untimely end by accidentally dropping a heavy weight onto his head while performing in his native Sweden.

The day after the last performance my father happened to be at the Railway Station attending to some aspect of his business, and had left the platform just as the Carlisle-bound 'eleven train' had just pulled out of the station heading north. Just outside the station Father had noticed a horse and cart which he knew were the property of one Geordie Reay, a local carter, Geordie was still watching the train as it gathered speed on its way to Carlisle.

"Now, Geordie" said Father cheerfully,"What's t'been doing?" "Oh Hello, Mr Kidd" replied Geordie without enthusiasm, "I've been carting the luggage of that concert party from wherever they've been staying".

"Oh!" said Father,"Hae they paid thee?" Father always had the knack of putting his finger on the nub of any problem like this. By this time the train was doing about thirty miles an hour and was almost half a mile on its way to Carlisle.

Geordie shook his head and replied mournfully,"Nut yit!"

Chapter 8

Marmara

We just *had* to call the boat that, for we had just returned from our trip to Istanbul on the Orient Express! First we had taken a train from Ostend to Vienna, where we stayed for two wonderful days. The whole place seemed friendly and surgically clean, and when we entered a small restaurant the waiter keenly looked us over. What he was doing was identifying our nationality, so that he could bring us the yesterday's editions of the English papers, before he had even taken our order! We left the wonderful capital for Budapest and Zagreb next morning promising an early return and a very much longer stay. But of course, life's like that. Full of broken promises! We've never been back.... but someday. The Iron-Curtain was still fully operational, and high barbed-wire fences could be seen stretching to the horizon on each side of the track.Our third-class compartment was full of Eastern European workers who were returning home after a year in the West. A vicious little gauleiter woman was going up and down the train sternly checking the papers of all these scared-looking migrants. When I tried some form of communication with some of them by drawing little sketches they looked terrified.

East of Budapest there were no dining cars. This was the *real* Orient Express! The one where you take your own toilet paper! There were still two full days to go. (Would we have enough?) As the train headed East, doing at least twenty five miles an hour at times, many of the small wayside stations had several elderly peasant women ready to sell fresh-baked loaves of bread, little bottles of plum brandy and baskets of eggs. When I tapped an egg gently on the side of the train, enquiringly, the old girl said "Ya ya! Gecüchd!" And so they were! But we had no salt. I leaned out of the window and took Polaroid photos of black water-buffaloes grazing a swamp. Odd little minarets. Picket

fences round the tidy houses, with their enormous piles of logs collected all ready for the winter to come, although it was only May. Everything was just a bit different. As we crawled along there was a pony and trap keeping pace with us. The work-ponies still have to work even when they are suckling their foals. You can see one doing just this in the "Doctor Zhivago" film. I carefully took a lovely Polaroid shot. Sadly, just as I pressed the button, the mare turned onto a side track, and so now, when I show the photo to anyone I have to say "The foal is just behind that bush!"

As we entered Bulgaria - then still ruled by the Communists - the train was boarded by a pair of rather ominous-looking, pistol-packing police who - for cash - sold us visas which the Bulgarian Embassy in London had assured us wouldn't be required. But we didn't feel like arguing. They also herded everyone who couldn't produce a valid vaccination certificate into a sort of platelayers hut, where the deficiency was made good by a man in a dirty looking white coat. Altogether this took about an hour.

Every little station displayed a large portrait of the communist dictator in a heroic pose. No one remembers his name now. There was a general air of depression. But about midnight a smiling attendant - the first for a hundred miles - opened the door and said "Welcome to Turkey!" And in a couple of hours we were in wonderful, fascinating, welcoming Istanbul.

When we checked-in at the Pera Palace Hotel and remarked to the staff of the incident at the station where a breathless railway worker - who had discovered our camera which we had inadvertently left on the rack - rushed up to the barrier with my Polaroid. "Oh" said the receptionist,"these sort of incidents are quite common. We often get taxi-drivers who call in to ask if any of our clients have left something of value which they've discovered in their cab!"

The bridges across the Bosforus hadn't yet been completed. We were pleased about that, for taking a ferry to Asia seemed so much more glamorous. A small boy had carried his work as a bootblack onto the ferry and wanted to polish my shoes. He brushed aside my reservations about my suedes. 'O.K' he said.

'Special stuff', and promptly got on with it, without waiting. While he was hard at work my wife took his photograph with the Polaroid, and by the time he had finished, it had 'developed'. When the boy saw the photo he was fascinated with it and offered all his meagre takings if he could buy it. We took another for him but somehow it wasn't quite the same as the original.

So our boat was duly renamed "Marmara"! A twenty-eight foot former ship's lifeboat, lying in the large basin at Glasson Dock. My old teenage stamping ground. There had been hours, days, probably even years, of loving work put into the boat by its owner, a Liverpool bus driver. He probably had never had the time to take his pride and joy to sea. There was a tiny cabin with two berths, even a little 'loo', a wheelhouse, and an engine which ran on vaporising oil. And a reddish steadying sail although with only a token keel we didn't suppose that it would sail into the wind. But the world was our oyster. Well - say - the Irish Sea! But first we would try our boating skills, which had last been used on my canvas boat in Northern Ireland all those years ago. We would go up onto the Lancaster and Preston Canal! This meant we had to use the locks, eight of which would have to be negotiated. There was actually something quite fascinating about the first lock. The old wooden doors, straining under the weight of hundreds of tons of canal water, some of which was shooting through every orifice.

The second lock was almost equally enjoyable. But when we finally emerged onto the canal proper it was with the unspoken knowledge that we would have all those eight or ten locks to manage all over again on the way back. We began to yearn for the relatively open sea.

The whole idea of the canal was to acquire sufficient boatmanship to eventually take "Marmara" onto tidal waters and in time, the Irish Sea, and to a little fishing village on the Whithorn peninsula, where we owned a small week-end cottage. In fact it was a former 'pre-fab' which had been given a coat of 'rough-cast' in a feeble and unsuccessful attempt to disguise its lowly origin.

The great day came when I felt confident enough to take a couple of friends fishing off-shore. There was a strong breeze and as we rounded the point, I could foresee that it might be a little uncomfortable, to say the least, at the chosen spot where flounders were supposed to actually jump into one's boat.

We dropped anchor and I almost immediately felt a little queasy, but the intrepid anglers maintained that they had often fished in far rougher waters. I retired again to the relative warmth and comfort of one of the bunks and eventually dropped off into an uneasy sleep. At length I roused myself. There was no sound save for the creaking of the timbers and the lashing of the now considerable sea. When I looked out, one of the seasoned fishermen was quite green as he puked over the edge. The other was holding his rod grimly in one hand and holding his dentures in the other. Neither seemed to object when I told them I was 'going in'.

Back on land they seemed to recover somewhat,and when I pointed out that in all conscience they couldn't go home empty-handed, they got me to pull up at a local fish-shop. One emerged with local caught plaice, which would be ideal for his unscrupulous and dishonest deception, but the other intrepid angler had bought two pounds of Finnan-Haddock! At our village swimming gala the next day, the sight of the rippling water was enough to send the Finnan-Haddock man hastily to the toilet block

Eventually, after several pleasurable months, my mentor said that he felt that as long as he and his crew-mate came along we could go on the first convenient tide. Pamela would drive the car to Whithorn following the A76 Stranraer road a hundred miles round South-west Scotland and turn off South down the peninsula to the Isle of Whithorn and would be waiting at the cottage for us to arrive after our marathon twenty four hour trip, and then ferry us home.

The historic trip itself was uneventful. By the time we were out of sight of Black Coombe Fell, north of Barrow, we could just see the Isle of Man. We pulled in to Ramsey, and phoned a progress report. Pam would be at the cottage waiting for us at our ETA about mid-day the next day.

After an unremarkable voyage we made our landfall and made all secure on our new mooring and then got a lift to the cottage where we had breakfast and settled down to wait for Pam. Hours later there was a noise of a car pulling up. I roused myself, for it didn't sound like Pam's car. And it wasn't. She got out of the strange car looking like a very dishevelled tramp. Bursting into tears in my arms, she told all she could of the accident.

Just short of Bladnock distillery - the most southerly in Scotland - and rather surprisingly, actually further south than Carlisle - she had either had a puncture, or had maybe fallen asleep. We'll never know. The car had ploughed through a hedge and then turned over as it fell a full ten or twelve feet, landing upside down in a small bog! This must have acted as an efficient shock-absorber. She hadn't got her seat-belt fastened which might have been just as well, and after recovering her senses was able to wind open a window - for the doors were immovable - and crawl out through the bog,and then climb up the steep bank to the road. Several cars drove past as she waved frantically for help, but as there was no sign whatever of a broken-down car, or an accident even, the drivers evidently decided that it would be unwise to risk stopping for such an apparition. However,eventually, a Good Samaritan pulled up and after verifying that there was, in fact, a car down there, he climbed down and switched off the ignition and recovered Pam's handbag, before bringing her to the cottage. Then he went home to change!

There was no alternative to hiring a car to get home. Somehow we never thought of sailing 'Marmara' back to England! For Pam and I would be leaving for Scotland again as soon as we looked presentable. Our old car was maybe fated to be written-off. But it was the night of the Potato Marketing Boards' Annual Dinner at Peebles Hydro. We extended the hire agreement for a week or two because the wrecked car was indeed confirmed as a complete 'write-off'

I had been elected some years earlier as one of the four Marketing Board Members to represent the then six Northern Counties, although the vast majority of the six thousand commercial potato growers were in Lancashire and Yorkshire, only one or two in

Westmorland, while Cumberland and Northumberland had about five hundred. However many of us were growing Certified Seed Potatoes under the same strict regime as obtained in Scotland. My Farmers Union branch went as far as to nominate me for the election, and then I was 'on my own.' But unless I could get a substantial number of particularly Lancashire and Yorkshire votes, the attempt was doomed!

The only way to reach the electorate was by post, so I formulated a pithy election address pointing out where the Board was failing. It was actually succeeding in many of its aspects. But where it failed was unmercifully pointed out in my address. I also had the good fortune of being ranged in a television debate with the Board Chairman, and was considered, at least by my friends, as having won the debate by a clear margin. As a very small grower myself I hoped to gain the support of all the 'small-men' as well as substantial numbers of the larger growers. It would be necessary to augment my personal arguments about the Board's 'failures' in a comprehensive 'Election Address' posted to all the Northern Area's seven thousand growers.

The problem which I clearly saw, would be in actually persuading these growers firstly to open the envelope. And then to read the contents of my hard-hitting Election Address. About half the letters which drop through one's letter-box are consigned instantly to the waste paper basket, and I didn't want this to happen with my quite expensive message. For my postage costs alone were several hundred pounds! So I recruited all my female friends and relatives and got them to address the envelopes. By hand! A female 'hand' would ensure that if the recipient himself didn't open the envelope - under a very suspicious eye - then his wife would do it for him! I even considered that a whiff of perfume might have a similar effect. It must have worked, for in spite of the odds I was duly elected, and I subsequently served on the Board for sixteen years.

Although not written into the Board's constitution, the dinner was an opportunity for the hierarchy of Scottish potato growers and members of the Scottish Farmers Union to say their pieces. And maybe just a touch long windedly, although none seemed to last more than forty minutes. Over the years the dinner had become a rather dull affair, especially for the ladies. So I had argued but without success, that we should give the event a more social aspect, perhaps even having a 'bit of a dance'! All my arguments had been in vain.

We arrived at the Hydro in time for the dinner, which was as good as ever. But before the speeches started I ushered Pam solicitously from the dining room. We found a little bar somewhere and had a very pleasant evening.

The Board meeting proper took place next morning. Most people imagine that there is nothing much to get steamed-up about, if I can use that phrase, in 'potatoes', of all things! But there were the annual hundred and ten thousand tons of potatoes from Cyprus, which had arrived just as the British early-potato season was getting into its stride, and due to a short winter, a mild winter, or a hundred other unforseen factors, the British potato grower was having a raw deal. Then there were the Reports, the Legal Committee, the Basic-Area-Committee, Market Reports. And so on. It dragged on quite a bit.

At last, it seemed, the Board's publicity efforts were paying-off. For the first time each member of the greater British public was eating over a hundred pounds of potatoes a year. We were now eating more than the Germans. It all had to be talked about. It took all morning.

Finally the Board Chairman, a dour, rather humourless potato grower from Fife called the last item on the Agenda. "Any other business!" I seized the chance to have one more try. “Mr Chairman!" I said gravely, "I would very much like to take this opportunity of apologising to you, Sir, and members of the Board for any apparent discourtesy last night, at the Annual Dinner when my wife and I had to leave the dinner before the speeches had started." I paused. I had the full attention of the Board. Then I went on."I'm sure that most Board members know by now that my wife was involved in a very serious road accident at the week-end." I paused again. I didn't want anyone to miss it. I swallowed and went on. "She is very lucky to be alive,and it may take some time for her to recover from the effects. In fact", I said with emphasis," she reared up in bed last night screaming 'Get me out! Get me out!'. She seemed absolutely terrified. I put my arm around her and tried to comfort her. "But you aren't in the car now, darling! You are **not in the car**" I repeated, slowly and distinctly. "No!" she replied, "It isn't the car I'm thinking about! It's the speeches!"

The Board meeting dissolved, almost in tears. Even the Chairman was seen to smile, albeit rather grimly. As we left the Hydro, people were still laughing. But the following year we **did** have a little dance afterwards!

Chapter 9

In Line For An Iron Cross?

There have been very few times, since the day I was shipwrecked on Will Pool, when I have been without a boat of some sort, and I couldn't see any reason why it should be any different simply because I was in the Army. Particularly so when there was an enormous Lough within a mile of our County Down camp at Loughbrickland. So I made a large canvas boat. It was too big to call a canoe for it had an eleven foot mast and a beam of five feet and a length of fifteen feet. My long-suffering mother somehow ran-up a sail to suit these dimensions. I almost believed a local character in the "Seven Stars" pub when he said my boat had out paced his trotting horse and trap, along the mile stretch of the road where it borders the side of the Lough. However he had the reputation of having an enormous thirst, so I ignored his empty glass.

But it had been when I was looking for a suitable bit of canvas that the germ of the idea entered my head. Coming back from Belfast one Saturday night with twenty other 'rude and licentious soldiery' in what was always termed the 'passion-waggon', I looked up enviously at the camouflaged canvas sheet above us. Then I thought, it would be so simple, to simply invert the tubular metal frame and the canvas sheet, and hey-presto, you would have a boat!

After a few sketches and diagrams, and an attempt to work out the buoyancy, I was convinced that the idea was feasible, and got someone to type out my explanatory screed, and addressed it to the Commanding Officer.

To my surprise I was sent for the same day and invited to elaborate on my idea. After closely questioning me, he authorised me the use of a thirty hundredweight truck 'for experimental purposes', together with six or seven of my close mates for crew. He would come down to the lough at ten o'clock on Saturday morning and have a look at the thing.

The idea needed a bit of refining, but the boat worked all right, drawing only a few inches of water, but there was nowhere to stand, except with some difficulty,on the tubular metal framework of what was now the 'floor'. The paddles were very good. Couldn't have been better.They were 'shovels, general-purpose', obtained with some difficulty from the Regimental Quartermaster's stores. They were a sort of cross between a shovel and a spade, and made ideal paddles. Three paddlers at each side gave an adequate speed. The lack of a floor was solved by throwing a few bed-boards across the tubular frame; but at a pinch we could manage without.

Colonel Reid, a regular officer, came down to the loch with Edward Bowers, as promised, on the Saturday morning and seemed somewhat surprised, not to say somewhat annoyed, that the three-ton Bedford was parked near the water's edge, apparently still unprepared for the little demonstration. As I saluted I asked the Colonel if he would mind timing the whole 'conversion' procedure.

Naturally we had taken every precaution to ensure that all went without a hitch. The nuts and bolts securing the tubular metal frame which supported the canvas sheet, had been discreetly oiled, and we had made sure that an extra spanner or two of the appropriate size were ready in the pockets of the four 'crewmen' who would be responsible for removing the frame from the lorry body, while the others removed the canvas sheet and spread it out tidily ready for the next stage.

The frame was then inverted and laid in the middle of the canvas, while I fastened a length of signal wire firmly round what would now become the uprights and secured it tightly. Then the canvas sheet was lifted up, and over, this wire and made fast to any convenient part of the frame. This was the boat! It was lifted quite easily by four men and launched. As a bit of a refinement we had borrowed a few bed-boards from the Quartermaster's Stores, and

laid them across the metal frame of what was now the floor. Six of us carried the thing and placed it in the water. The Colonel looked at his watch and beamed. "Four minutes, Kidd!" he said, smiling, "Right! Let's get aboard!"

The boat exceeded my expectations, and with this initial load drew only about four or five inches of water. I had three of the 'crew' at each side to act as paddlers, and of course I was captain! We paddled round the nearest island and headed back to the launching site. The boat was absolutely stable and I steered by orders to the paddlers.

The colonel was enormously enthusiastic, and struck with the possibilities. 'Four minutes! Edward." he said excitedly, "A boat in four minutes! We must show this to the C.R.A." He was referring to the Brigadier who was in command of all the Division's artillery regiments.

So started a whole summer of demonstrating the boat. The C.R.A was equally enthusiastic, as was his corresponding head of our 197 Infantry Brigade. Then of course, the Divisional Commander, a Major-General, had to have his turn. He quizzed me about how I envisaged the use of the boat.

My thinking was that, provided some personnel in each regiment were trained in its use, the boat could be of enormous use. Any inland water obstacle would be a barrier no longer if there were canvas lorry-tops to be had. And after use they could be replaced on the lorries almost as quickly. Another advantage, I said, was that that they were less detectable to aerial reconnaisance than the Royal Engineer's conventional boats.The General seemed impressed. "I'm going to push this idea!" he said.

So a combined visit from the Lt.General, Commanding B.T.N.I. - British Troops, Northern Ireland - was imminent. And with him would be his equivalent ranking officer, the Lt.General commanding all Royal Artillery in the U.K.

The big demo was to be held on a reservoir near Rathfriland. There would be the two Lieutenant-Generals, then the Divisional commander, a Major-General, as well as three or four assorted Brigadiers, plus of course our own Colonel Grant. He had recently replaced Colonel Reid who had gone on somewhere to higher command. The second-in-command and of course Edward,the adjutant, brought up the rear. So it was a pretty high-powered party which debouched from their staff cars at the lough side. My team had been kitted up with brand new tropical shorts and plimsols for the occasion.

As the officers debouched from their staff-cars and strolled over the shingle towards us, I brought up 'my' men and saluted. To my considerable surprise everybody piled in the boat, without discussion. I therefore immediately eased the boat gently off the shingle before jumping aboard.

With over twenty men aboard, the boat swept along quite comfortably. The staff-car drivers, settled down to have a natter and a smoke by their cars. All was going very smoothly. Then I realised that our high 'freeboard' and twenty odd standing personel constituted a very effective 'sail' indeed, which accounted for our remarkable speed. And also it was evident, at least to me, that with only six paddlers, we couldn't hope to get back to the starting point, as expected.

It was a time for a rapid decision, and I took it. Cupping my hands, I bawled out in an authoritative sort of accent which possibly could have sounded like one acquired at Sandhurst, "Go round to the other side!" The drivers acknowledged, and extinguishing their cigarettes, made for their cars and set off for the 'other side'.

We reached the opposite side of the Lough almost as the small convoy of staff-cars arrived; just in time! My very distinguished passengers all disembarked, quite excitedly, full of praise and with very warm congratulations.

Later on I began to think that there might easily have been some sort of posthumous decoration from the Wermacht, for there hadn't been a single life jacket on board. Maybe an Iron Cross! Six British Generals and a Colonel in one go!

But I never heard any more about the idea. Not a sausage! It was really most disappointing. But almost twenty years later as I went to the bookstall on Euston station before returning from a Potato Marketing Board meeting, my eye caught sight of the Army Magazine "Soldier". On the front was a caption; "Can you recognise this boat?" The photo showed some Engineer cadets with what was undoubtedly *my* boat! I wrote to their correspondence columns claiming that not only could I recognise it, but that I had invented the thing, and gave corroborative details.

Some months later I had a letter from the Commander of the then Ceylon army, in Columbo; Brigadier Reid, our old colonel. And for some years we carried on a correspondence. He was even kind enough to send me his Christmas card showing Her Majesty the Queen and Prince Phillip with him in his jeep reviewing the troops. Later he urged me to put in a claim to the Commission which was making awards to war-time inventors. Whatever the Mr Bailey recieved (the man who invented the bridges) he richly deserved every penny. On that basis I thought I might possibly receive, say, a hundred pounds or so. However the Commission had to have details of where the 'invention' had been used before making any award. And I wasn't in a position to get such information, so obviously the claim lapsed.

Some years later however, I met a former Colonel in the Royal Marines who said that my boats had been most useful on the Chindwin! But by then the Royal Commission on Awards to Inventors had ceased operations!

There was another footnote however when I saw some Territorials actually using the boat on my own River Eden. I went down to the gravel bed and spoke to the subaltern in charge, and told him the story. He was fascinated and rummaged somewhere in his kit and produced what I think was called "*The Infantry Manual of Rafting, Boating, and Bridging*". The text of the chapter about the boats was, I felt sure, my original text that I had sent in to my Colonel all those years ago!

Chapter 10

Driving Down to Kent

We were to drive down to Kent. The whole Regiment. With our guns and waggons we were shipped over from Belfast to Stranraer, and we made Carlisle before nightfall. The Regiment was housed overnight, as Roman Legions were so many centuries before, in "Hadrian's Camp". With my parents living only fifteen miles away I felt confident that I would somehow be able to slip away and sneak a visit home, but alas, there wasn't a chance! We were virtually prisoners.

Next day we had an early start and were set off in small convoys of about twelve or fifteen vehicles, in order to keep any congestion to the minimum. The R.S.M. - always referred to as "Tara", (from the North-Country use of the apostrophe T; i.e."T'aresem") brought up the rear of our section. Sometimes quite descriptive adjectives were attached to his name.

We drove steadily down the - to me - familiar stretches of the A6. I was pleased we were going at the regulation twenty miles in the hour because I had been detailed to drive the only Austin three ton truck in the regiment. It had the great disadvantage of having no windscreen but instead had a small canvas screen which could be pulled up and, hopefully, fastened under ones's chin in bad weather. Within twenty miles my face was bright red. Until relatively recently the A6 road was always termed "The Military". That name too, was harking back to the Roman Legions. A few miles on we climbed a long curving slope which many of the older generation still called "Thiefside". It was believed that this was where, as the horses were slowed down by the hill, the highwaymen would pounce, with "Stand and deliver!" As we neared the turn-off to my village of Lazonby, three miles away, I pulled up on the grass verge and quickly lifted the bonnet enquiringly as Tara slowed down to see what was the matter. "No problem, Sir!" I yelled, "We'll catch you up in a few minutes!" He looked a bit suspicious and uncertain, but drove on. As soon as he was well out of sight we turned off the main road and drove for home.

Alas for our plans, the birds had flown! No one at home. The garage was empty. But,'in for a penny', we thought, and drove on another two miles to Kirkoswald and Fog Close Farm. My sister Margaret was staggering across the farmyard with a bucket of boiling water, followed at a safe distance by her little daughter Anne. It was pig-killing day. The deed had just been done and now large quantities of boiling water were required to enable the butcher to scrape the quite surprising amounts of hair from the recumbent carcase. For Young Dunk, my co-driver,the age-old scene was a revelation. Like most urban dwellers he had only vague ideas about the need - if meat is to be eaten - to kill animals. He looked slightly shocked by this important discovery, but recovered sufficiently to be able to relieve Margaret from the task of water carrying so that she could put the frying pan on the Aga, and while we watched the butcher and heard the news about lambing time from Alan, my brother in law - who had turned up from the lambing shed - she quickly fried bacon and eggs for our 'ten o'clocks'. Then we were loaded up with off-the-ration delicacies like eggs, ham,sausages and home made cakes, and then we had to bid farewell, for we had 'lost' more than half an hour.

The rest of our section had evidently stopped somewhere on route, for we slipped back into our place just on the old Westmorland-Lancashire border, trying our best to avoid looking smug as we overook Tara. But to my astonishment, a few miles further on, standing on the side of the road, was the familiar figure of my mother and another woman! She was an aunt who lived nearby, and with whom Mother had decided to spend a few days. In a flash I realised what had happened. Margaret must have phoned to my aunt's house, to urge them to 'get down to "Carnforth Level" where, hopefully, they would be able to wave to us at least, as the convoy passed. As Mother and I kissed, Tara looked on unbelievingly as his waggon swept on. But he must have been human after all, for after my explanation he never mentioned it again. He had accepted half a pound of sausages, so his hands were somewhat tied.

In another three days we had arrived at Folkestone, to see for the first time enemy-held territory, across the twenty-odd miles of the English Channel. It was Saint Patrick's Day. As we gazed across the calm waters we could just discern a trail of white smoke, evidently from a locomotive nearing Calais. Enemy territory! As if to emphasise the point, a shell from one of the huge cross-channel guns on Cap Gris Nez landed about two hundred yards out to sea and threw up a huge column of water, followed a moment or two later by the sound of the explosion. It had taken four years to get this far.

Wet behind the ears

A young subaltern, still wet behind the ears, who had only just arrived at R.H.Q. straight from school and OCTU, ostensibly to fill the post (if indeed there was one so low), of assistant to the assistant-adjutant, decided that it was high time that us 'layabouts had a bit of marching drill'. We were a slack lot, he said. So the Orderly Sergeant was instructed to have us ready for some old-fashioned square bashing. It would do us a lot of good.

The lad marched us up and down, halted us, about-turned us, double-marched us and was clearly enjoying himself. Then he tried us with a few 'to your front-salute's!' We still remembered this odd manoeuvre, strangely enough, from our early days four years before. On the order, "To your front - wait for it! - Salute!" we were supposed to halt, 'two three', salute, 'two three', 'about turn, 'two three', and then march briskly back in the opposite direction.

Unfortunately the young man had left it a bit late in giving the command. He had allowed us to get well over a hundred yards away before he gave the order. There was a very strong breeze indeed blowing off the Channel but those in the rear of the column heard the order all right and executed the manoeuvre beautifully and then marched smartly back towards the young man.

Sadly there was some confusion with the rest of the column. Those who were in the middle thought that he had shouted "Halt!". So they halted. Well, nearly all of them. But those at the front never heard him at all. So they marched on unknowingly, hoping he would say something before they marched into the sea. Utter confusion is perhaps an understatement.

The Orderly Sergeant was sent running until he, at least, was in earshot, and eventually he managed to restore some sort of order and marched us all back to the starting point and the angry young man who subjected us to a quite remarkable flow of invective. For one so young he had acquired an amazingly extensive vocabulary and used every word. Then he ordered us to about-turn, and then 'double marched' us up the precipitous slope behind. Twice. He was like the grand old Duke of York himself. Then he addressed us. He had quite a good turn of phrase. He kept on and on. He was unrelenting. Eventually as he paused for breath, Young Dunk came to attention in the fashion immortalized in "*Dad's Army*". Like Lance-Corporal Jones he said "Permission to speak, Sir!"

The young subaltern, 2nd Lieutenant Marshall, was still red in the face with fury. "What the hell do *you* want?" he barked, as menacingly as he could, "Excuse me, Sir, we couldn't hear your word of command, Sir" said Young Dunk bravely, "because of the wind and the crunching of our feet on the gravel." "Hell's bells!", snorted the subaltern,angrily,"why don't you wash your bloody ears out!" "Well Sir" replied Young Dunk, unwisely, "I wash my ears out just as often as you do, Sir!" Young Marshall exploded. "March this man away, Sergeant, and put him on a charge of insolence to an officer!" And so Dunk was marched away between two of his erstwhile fellow marchers, and lodged in the Guardroom under close arrest.

Next morning he was marched under escort, in front of the acting C.O. The second-in-command was Major Sykes, a career officer who subsequently made Brigadier. He professed to be outraged. "In thirty years service", he said, "I've never had to try a case like this! Insolence to an officer!" He paused as if to control himself." However, in view of an official letter of complaint about certain events, I'm reluctantly going to dismiss the charge! March him out, and send Mr Marshall in!"

As I listened to Young Dunk relating his amazing escape, I reflected that I had put paid to any lingering hope of promotion. Next day Marshall was posted to one of our three batteries, which were lodged in the Shorncliffe barracks. They had proper facilities for marching drill. Generations of troops had acquired there the fallen arches and flat feet which would fit them for serious soldiering.

The whole regiment moved to Salisbury Plains where we were to fire live rounds onto previously prepared slit-trenches and command posts and then later inspect the results of the barrage and calculate how many of us would have survived if we had actually been in our positions. We had toiled in the hot sun and blistering remarks of the R.S.M. to prepare a sound Regimental Command-Post. The chalk wasn't good to handle but eventually we managed to hack out a reasonably large-sized 'room' with recesses for shelves, and a large rectangular chalk 'table'. It looked quite impressive, but as we roofed it with branches before throwing more chalk on top I unwisely expressed my view that the roof timbers were not strong enough for the job. Tara angrily swore that he would be the man who would take such decisions.

The Colonel went round to inspect the Headquarters preparations for the barrage and had just emerged from the Command Post with his little retinue, pronouncing himself delighted with the work. As he congratulated the hovering R.S.M. on the way he had organised the whole thing and especially the command post with its little ledges forming chalk 'shelves', and said "The 'map-table' was marvellous", the effect was somewhat spoiled, just as the Colonel completed his remarks, by the sudden and total collapse of the roof.

It could have been an extremely serious incident. "I told you that those timbers weren't strong enough, Kidd!" shouted Tara angrily in my direction. It had actually been the other way round, and Tara had poured scorn on my warnings but I knew it was pointless opening my mouth.

Over the wall behind our wagon lines a lovely Guernsey herd was grazing, and that night I bought a week old heifer calf to start my farming career. Furze Hill Coral 75510, was to found a herd. She was sent home by rail to Cumberland, in a sack with her head sticking out. Within a week I had bought another three and sent them to my brother-in-law at Fog Close Farm to await my return from the war.

Chapter 11

The Hound Trail

Of course there is betting at hound trails. Everybody knows that. But the niceties of the sport are mysteries to most people except those who live in the fairly small area where the sport takes place. This is mainly in Cumberland and Westmorland (for most of the trail devotees have never accepted the Heath Walker plans) and those areas of Scotland which drain into the Solway Firth.

The basic principle is simple. Two volunteers take the 'drags', which are usually a sack, well soaked in aniseed, with a number of other 'secret' pungent ingredients, and trailing this on a short cord, runs, trots, or walks the circuitous route chosen by the committee, sometimes as much as ten or twelve miles over what is often scenery of wild mountain splendour. When he almost reaches 'home' the trail hounds, waiting with unbridled excitement are released to follow the trail which has been laid by the other volunteer and after they are safely away, the other 'drag' is brought in from the opposite direction to the finishing line. In the meantime the hounds are mostly out of sight of the spectators, but in hilly country may be seen from time to time, maybe a mile or two away, only just visible with the aid of powerful binoculars. Those with bets made are getting more and more excited and this excitement reaches a deafening climax when the first dogs appear in the finishing straight. This is the signal for a cacophony of shrieks and whistles which the owners fervently hope will encourage their own dog to make a last powerful effort to be first across the line. Now and again the frustration of some owners can be intense, when their particular dog - with a comfortable lead - sits down and scratches its behind only yards away from the finish.

On the whole it is a well run sport with strict rules. One rule, worked out by the governing body, with the full support of the

National Farmer's Union, is that if a hound goes missing - and it goes without saying that the hounds are big powerful and potentially dangerous animals to farm stock - then all further trails will be banned until that hound is accounted for. But from time to time rules can be bent or even broken. "It's the money, you see, what does it." said one wiseacre in explanation of the few rule infringements which do take place. Few people remember a dog which won large sums of money for its owner, a well known local business man. Sadly he blotted his copy-book when he was caught giving his hound a lift in his car over part of the course. He pleaded in vain that he was only acting as any animal lover would have done in the circumstances."Banned for life!" was the verdict of the outraged committee.

The new Co-op manager's son had never seen a hound trail, when his family arrived in the village and he couldn't possibly afford to go, when a hound-trail was scheduled for the Long Meadow at Scale Rigg. At least, not by the official entrance! The cheaper alternative was to watch the race from an old knarled oak tree near the dipping pens in Scale Rigg yard. It wouldn't be very comfortable but it was free!

The old Co-op manager had left the village under a cloud when his integrity had been challenged at a members' half-yearly meeting. The meeting had been adjourned until an investigation could take place. Unfortunately, however there had been a destructive fire in the Society's office, causing much of the possibly incriminating evidence to be destroyed and the manager had done a moonlight flit.

Ronnie settled into the lower boughs of the tree as he could hear the hounds 'giving mouth'. They had raced almost completely round Lazonby Fell and by the sound, Ronnie calculated that they would be racing under the tree in only minutes. The man with the finishing drag had trotted past soon after Ronnie climbed into a comfortable vantage point.

He could hear the raucous cries of the bookies, down in the Meadow. They were still taking bets. Suddenly he heard the sound of a motor-bike, and then he saw it stop right underneath him. He froze. He felt that it had all been a mistake. The bike had a sidecar attached and the two occupants took up positions on each side of the narrow lane. There was something about them he didn't like. The leading hound appeared, going like a racing greyhound. It was well clear of the second hound which was about a hundred yards behind. At the critical moment the tense men below the tree sprang out with enormous determination and agility and secured a tight grip on the leading hound and somehow managed to hang on to the struggling animal until the second hound had passed and was well on his way to the finishing tape. Then the men released their captive which immediately took up the trail again. The driver started up the motor-bike and they were off the same way as they had come. The whole operation had taken only three minutes.

At the finishing line the dog handlers shouted themselves hoarse, or whistled the distinctive whistles which they hoped their dogs would recognise. All of them had little canisters of their dog's favourite food ready to use as rewards.

Ronnie felt quite shaken, as he climbed down the tree and made his way to the finishing line where celebrations were in progress. The race officials listened intently to his tale and declared the race void. An enquiry was held and in the course of time the miscreants stood in the dock at the County Court where they were awarded long terms of imprisonment.

Acknowledgement
The pictures on pages 74 and 76 are reproduced by kind permission of Cumberland News, Carlisle.

Chapter 12

Mauks in mi Poddish

Most of us in the village believed that old Frank was quite deaf. This was because Frank always shouted, as many deaf people seem to do at times. But he was always the same. He always shouted. As regards his 'deafness', I know that he could hear the kitten-like mewing of a hunting buzzard, several hundred yards away. And if somebody in the noisy bar of the Joiners Arms said gently "Another one, Frank?" he seemed to hear well enough.

Nevertheless, he invariably shouted. He would start a one-sided conversation at a hundred yards distance. Once - after he became a widower - it was alleged that on a busy market day he proposed to an elderly but attractive widow, from across the road! When he was twelve, his hard-pressed mother had fixed him up with his first job, on a farm about ten miles away. Normally he would have gone to the hirings at Penrith, but he was a little under-sized, and looked a trifle younger than twelve so his mother thought that as the school-leaving age had now been raised to fourteen, "it would be better if he wasn't seen at the hirings".

Nearly all the farm workers, both male and female, presented themselves at the twice yearly hirings. The town was always crowded, with probably a circus, a fair, and cheapjacks of all descriptions. At the last fair, Frank's brother had been enlisted, for a promised sixpence, to assist "Professor Fox". For this promised reward all he had to do was to sit on a high seat, swathed in a white sheet, and hold his mouth open while the Professor Fox brandished a pair of shiny forceps over his head. In no time at all a small crowd would gather, hoping to see an extraction or even, with luck, an operation. As soon as the learned man judged that the crowd was sufficiently large, he would abandon the forceps and start his real business; selling patent-medicines.

At the hiring fair keen-eyed farmers would be using all their well-developed powers of observation to scan the crowds for a likely looking lad or lass. At some hirings a straw in the mouth advertised the fact that one was for hire. The 'grape-vine' would be busy for both sides. Farmers were being warned to keep off various unsuitable candidates, and men were warning each other to try and avoid noted "bad meat shops" where spartan diet was the order of the day. Virtually all young single men 'lived-in'; more or less with the family. Quite often, it was less. And so they naturally moved on after a six-month trial. Others stayed for the rest of their working lives; some marrying the daughter of the house.

Nearly seventy years later Frank described his first day at work, and something still rankled. He turned over the wad of "Black Twist" in his mouth and spat accurately but without malice at an inoffensive cat about six feet away. "Aye, we gits done-up, we gits iverything fed, awe t'coos milked foddered an mucked oot, an we gas in't hoose aboot ten to seven. Ah sups mi poddish - mauks 'n all - an ah sits an waits."

In point of fact, the "mauks" in Frank's "poddish" wouldn't have been 'mauks', (Cumbrian dialect for maggots) at all - but were probaby weevils or mealworms, a different thing altogether. At that time all the farm workers drank their tea from the same basin which they had used for their porridge.

Frank turned over the wad of tobacco again and continued his tale; "Ah sups mi poddish and sits and waits. But nowt appened!. What's thou waiten for?" said t'boss. "Ahs waiten for me tea!" 'ah ses, gai sharp! "Thou gits nea tea here wid thi breakfast!" he ses, mad- like.

But then the boss had apparently softened and went on in what was evidently a more conciliatory tone, "Thou nobbut gits tea wid thi poddish on Sundays."

When Frank first helped me to harvest, we were still using that marvellous fifty year-old machine, the binder. At the turn of the twentieth century this machine had fundamentally altered the

scene in the harvest field which had been virtually unchanged from biblical times. The McCormack binder actually cut and then tied the sheaves of golden corn! A machine called the "Reaper" had been used for a short period. But it didn't last for it couldn't tie the sheaves. Now the thousands of years of laboriously tying the sheaves with a "band" consisting of a handful long straws; unaltered since those biblical times, had ended.

There was something quite fascinating about sitting on the high driver's seat at the back of the machine and watching the cut oats falling onto the moving canvas, a wide canvas 'belt' which rapidly whisked them up, pressed between two more 'canvases' until a sheaf started bunching up behind the knotter. At regular intervals - pre-determined according to the size of sheaves required - two small arms whizzed round to sweep the bunched corn into a sheaf, which in the twinkling of an eye was tied with twine and ejected from the machine to await the stookers. Mr McCormack, the inventor was reputed to have been driven mad before he managed to perfect the knotting mechanism.

At harvest time Frank came to stook my corn, and his stooks, with their eight or ten sheaves stood firm, whatever the weather, for the three Sundays which were deemed necessary to 'harden the grain' before they were led away to the stack. As the binder progressed round and round the field, and the area of uncut corn became smaller and smaller with every circuit, the rabbits retreated to the uncut centre now getting visibly smaller in size with every circuit of the binder. Sudden rustles alerted the harvesters that at least one rabbit was determined to make a break for it. Sometimes dozens would be killed in wild chases over the stubble, which slowed them down and reduced the odds on their escape. On one memorable evening we had killed seventy.

And of course Frank taught me to make a stack, and to load a cart. It was a fearful humiliation if a stack 'slipped' and had to be rebuilt. And if a load of sheaves fell off the cart while on its way up the village it took a long time to live down.

In his early retirement; when he was seventy-five, I took Frank to a farm sale. These normally took place early in January so as to

A fiddle drill

facilitate the new tenants moving in on Candlemas day; the 2nd of February. The sale tradition hasn't changed much even today, although they now seem to take place at almost any time of year. The farm sale starts in the farmyard, which rapidly fills with prospective buyers and spectators. The auctioneer, quite often a new boy recently recruited to the profession finds a suitable vantage point on a farm trailer, or maybe on the granary steps, and the sale commences. Willing neighbours pass out a veritable treasure trove. An old war time Stirrup-Pump last used to whitewash the calf pens 'just after the war'. A couple of unopened crates of "Day's Black Draught" or "Vaccadine". Probably decades have elapsed since they were bought. They are probably a tribute to the persistence of some long forgotten patent-medicine salesman for they obviously hadn't been needed in the first place.

Some things, like scythes, cross-cut saws, hay rakes and other, now superseded items, are hard to clear. "Never mind" says the auctioneer briskly,"Put something else with them!" And the addition of, maybe, some mole traps, or that essential aid for a sheep farmer, a spade or maybe a 'geavalic', a crowbar, added to the unwanted item, would enable a sale to be made. A few ram's horns make a quite surprising amount from some walking-stick enthusiasts.

"Here is a fiddle drill!" It would have been worn on a strap round the neck of the user who would operate the bow of the "fiddle" thus actuating a small spinning disk which would evenly distribute the required amount of quite expensive grass seeds held in the canvas bag above the mechanism.They would be sent flying gently two to three yards on each side of the operator. The optimum amount of seed per acre was, and still is about thirty pounds per acre. Once the seeds had flown out from the disk they would have been virtually invisible on the soil so that the operator would need to keep his footsteps parallel to the ones which he had left on the previous trip across the field, so that the whole field was evenly covered with - hopefully - no unsown strips. The same principles in fact to that of the biblical sower of seeds.

Among the crowd, there is a substantial section of buyers who are only interested in bygones like this and the bids come fast and

Burdizzo Bloodless castrators ... maybe still another pair in the box

furious ending with a final bid which amazes the older generation who remember actually using what is now merely a curiosity.

Here was what might be an old surgical instrument. It is just that. It is an old, still shiny "Burdizzo" bloodless castrator! Someone held it up for inspection, and then made the crowd grin by holding the fearsome object threateningly in the proximity of the young auctioneer's genitals. As he retreats everybody laughs.

Frank and I had gone to the sale merely to enjoy the social aspects of such a gathering. We had no purchases in mind as we moved out to the field where the implements were lined up in the usual rows. By tradition "Lot One" is nearly always a large heap of scrap iron. Many of the items in the heap might still have some use, and men requiring any of this collection have to trade as best they can with real experts at trading; "the scrap men". Before they load up their old wagons they may already have sold enough small treasures from the heap to more than pay for it. And somehow or other they will probably be able to avoid the attentions of the taxman.

Next there are heaps of second or third-hand timber, followed by large numbers of hay racks and feed troughs. Among them some old stone troughs, which have anxious clients hovering near. More than likely, these troughs would have been the vessels in which the contents of bedroom chamber-pots were stored, to await daily collection by someone from the Kirkoswald blanket factory which operated until about 1900. The urine was much prized for its' ammonia content, and was used in processing the fleeces. The ardent bidders for these items, however, won't be aware of this unsavoury past as they struggle home with their weighty prizes which will adorn their gardens for years to come. An elderly voice could be heard telling how he once as a boy saw one of these sandstone troughs completed. "Aye, it took nearly awe day, and just as he gev it t'last la-al tap wid his hammer, he brock it!"

Frank went off on his own into the crowd but from time to time I could hear his raucous voice further up the lines. The man in command, the auctioneer, was pressing on for there was still a lot to sell and the 'lots' were almost imperceptibly increasing in value, until at last when he finally reached the end of the field where the tractors and modern implements were already attracting small crowds, everyone would return to the yard for the sale of the sheep and cattle.

Someone asked Frank how his wife was. She poor soul had ailed - on and off - for years. "Well," said Frank, hesitating,"Ah wish she'd git better or summat". A little later having separated from me, he spotted me from the other side of the crowd; there was his usual bawl. It was almost as if we hadn't travelled to the sale together! He had suddenly thought of something, "Will thi missus hev gitten back yit?" he shouted. Embarrassed, I hissed back "Yes!". "Oh thank you, Sir!," snapped the auctioneer smartly, "Malcolm Kidd! Twelve corn troughs! Twenty five shillings apiece!" Red-faced I moved away, vowing to keep my mouth shut unless I really wanted to buy something.

It was actually over a year later when Frank's wife died, and my brother Harold and I were among the bearers at the funeral. As farmers who would be "at home", that is, in the village anyway, we were often roped-in for these occasions. The church service over, we started to climb the extremely steep churchyard to where the open grave awaited the interment. We were following the local joiner, almost unrecognisable in his black undertaker's attire. The short grass made progress up the hill difficult and at times almost impossible. Harold, who was one of the two front bearers, breathlessly shot out from the corner of his mouth,to the undertaker "Git thi'sel a hint man, and shove!". The addition of a little more motive power enabled us to reach the open grave, and the committal took place.

This over, the four bearers stood back to allow the few family mourners to pay their last respects. But as Frank caught my eye from the other side of the open grave, he bawled out in his stentorian tones - obviously quite confident that he was speaking in a reverent whisper - "It's that steep up here, it's nobbut fit to bury bloody hantilopes!"

Chapter 13

The Way the Cookie Crumbles

We were a lucky regiment; there's no doubt about it. It had nothing to do with anything else but luck.How can one explain it, otherwise? There we were, willing - more or less - to be sent anywhere, at any time. But while "Y listed" men, who had been listed "sick" by virtue of being hospitalised for three weeks or more - were sent off to reinforcement units, and in many cases were posted off to units on the brink of overseas service - we continued our perambulations round most of the United Kingdom!

Then, on the 6th of June, while we were living in comparative comfort in the requisitioned boarding houses of Margate, the final phase started. When in due course our turn came, we drove in small convoys to the East India docks. We could see what Jerry had been doing to London. Now and again the Flying Bombs, the V1s, would be heard, with their sinister buzz. One flew towards the City, directly above our halted convoy. And when the buzzing stopped, we waited, with a sort of morbid fascination, to see just where and when it would abandon its glide and plunge to earth.

At the docks checks were made to see if all vehicles were properly 'waterproofed' - in case of a 'wet landing' on the beaches. I had a rather odd vehicle; a Hillman Minx wireless car, which for some reason couldn't be adequately 'waterproofed'. It was for Fred Cheetham the Captain-Quartermaser, a WW1 veteran who for some reason couldn't sit for long in any other Army vehicle. The waterproofing process involving keeping the water from all the 'electrics' of the vehicle with large amounts of 'gunge',and installing a 'breathing tube' to allow dry air to be drawn down into the carburettor. In theory this should allow a vehicle to be driven in four or five feet of water. I had been assigned to get this one over to Normandy for him. Fred was already over there. But a check of all vehicles' waterproofing was made at the docks. A white disc was painted on the wing indicating that the vehicle had been examined and properly prepared for a wet landing.The Hillman naturally failed the inspection but got a white disc just the same!

We were loaded on to Liberty ships. These vessels had been made to a uniform easy-build pattern in the U.S. They could turn them out in eight weeks. As we crossed the Channel the convoy left a trail of empty Compo boxes. Each box had contained all the rations which fourteen men would require for a twenty-four hour period. It also included what proved to be a rather inadequate amount of toilet paper. Everbody had to wear somewhat flimsy-looking inflatable Mae-West's at all times. "Mae West's chest was never like that!", said one keen-eyed observer.

There was a veritable Armada lying at anchor off Grey-sur Mere, where we were to land. Yet that word is woefully inadequate. The Spanish Armada wouldn't have filled a hundreth part of it; the enormous bay was chock-full. There seemed to be literally thousands of vessels of all description. Barrage balloons swayed in the breeze. Small naval vessels bustled about on urgent business. After waiting our turn for a day and a night, our vehicles were swung out and loaded into waiting landing craft and we climbed down the nets to join them.

To my dismay the Hillman Minx had been loaded right in the bows, below the ramp, which obscured the view of the beach ahead. Salt spray blew over like heavy rain. I fervently hoped that my engine would start first time, for if it failed, there would be a hiatus. I would be holding-up everybody, especially if we had a wet landing. An inquest would be inevitable. We all started-up and awaited the crunch.

There were no bullets flying. The front was some miles away. But when the craft settled gently onto the sandy beach, I was relieved to find that we had a completely dry landing. If we had had to wade through two or three feet of water, the Minx would have caused chaos. We swept off the beach in some disorder, past the Beachmaster, a real John Bull character with an enormous moustache and an encouraging grin. There was a proliferation of small tin signs varying from "Keep to the right!" to some in a strange script; "Achtäng. Minen!" with skull and crossbones to add emphasis. Had they been planted for their benefit or ours? Nobody seemed to know. Other more familiar signs enabled us to find firstly the Divisional area and eventually our own Regiment.

"Any bother about the Hillman, Kidd?" "No? Right!; you and Gosling will be taking the water truck from now on! Thus started my part - to quote the immortal Spike - in the liberation of Europe. In a new and quite mundane role. As long as everyone in the regiment had an adequate amount, usually a gallon or so, of filtered and chlorinated water per day, we were virtually left to our own devices. In contrast to previous military operations, where thousands, and quite often hundreds of thousands of fighting men were killed off by water- borne epidemics, this invasion was to be different. At least, practically nobody was to die of dysentery in this theatre of war.

The Royal Engineers had set-up watering points where enormous canvas tanks of filtered and chlorinated water were available to a constant stream of water-trucks. (All water-trucks, however could pump, filter and treat their own supply, from any suitable river or stream). On returning to ones' unit, troops came and collected their own requirements. Everyone seemed to have their own bucket. Home made ones, with the top cut off from a discarded 'non returnable' petrol tin, in which they collected their daily requirement from the row of taps at the rear of the vehicle. PLUTO; (pipe-line under the ocean) hadn't yet started to operate but there never was a shortage of petrol.

The Infantry divisions were fighting slowly inland and were now in ideal country for the stubborn German defenders, who used the 'bocage' country of small fields with their frequent high hedges on thick earthwork banks, to the very best advantage. Every day and every hedge brought a fierce infantry battle. Every hedge or cider-apple orchard made ideal defensive positions which had to be bitterly fought for. Meanwhile the tank battles, south-east of

Examining ditched and abandoned Tiger tank

Caen,were proving that German tanks had a considerable superiority over ours. One German tank ace destroyed over sixteen British tanks in ten horrific minutes at Villers Bocage. We drove quickly, past the red-rusted Shermans every day. Knocked-out tanks which had been on fire, rusted red in only a few days.

The recognised ratio of losses was that it took the sacrifice of two out of three Shermans at least, to knock out a German Tiger. In forward areas, smouldering tanks, still with the remains of their incinerated crews, bore witness to this. Normandy cows lay bloated with their feet in the air. Some were still to be shot, and I often got this job myself after Fred Cheetham ignored my warning that he was aiming his revolver at the wrong spot. He pointed right between the eyes of a wounded horse, and seemed amazed after the shot,when it still stood looking at him. "All right, Kidd! You do it then; you're a farmer's boy!"

German tanks were very much better than ours. Spandau machine guns better than our Bren guns, Schmeiser machine pistols better than Sten guns, and multi- barrelled mortars, were all far better than ours. The PBI; 'Poor Bloody Infantry', suffered greviously for British politicians' failures to see that our infantry were provided with the best. Somebody should have been shot for sending our boys out with inferior material.

But our artillery was better by far. It was said that some captured enemy general asked if he could have a look at the British "automatic field guns". Our guns were lethal. By the middle of August, our twenty-five pounders had to have new barrels. They had fired hundreds of thousands of rounds. But in eight weeks, our Divisional infantry had been decimated. Not for nothing had they called themselves the P.B.I.

The extraordinary thing was that German artillery was relatively feeble, compared to ours. In very many cases - to our surprise - it was actually horse drawn and wheels had solid tyres! Thick-set stocky horses were the motive power. Breeds of horses we had never seen before, possibly bred for meat, for they were very well fleshed.

New barrels in a twenty-five pounder

A more mundane problem arose with the truck. Our L.A.D. (Light Aid Detachment) of the R.E.M.E. said that the engine was done. They used a more technical word for it! The engine would have to be replaced by a new one at Divisional Workshops. I was given a map reference and told to 'take it gently and it might get there under its own power'. I duly reported with the truck and was told to 'keep out of the way and pick it up in twenty-four hours'.

The Orne had been crossed a day or two before, by units of our own 59th Division. Thury Harcourt, a very small town, a little way upstream, had had ninety per cent of its houses badly damaged or destroyed by the bombing and shelling. Forty-four civilians had been killed. But almost every year since the war, veterans of the Division have attended commemorative services in the Parish Church and the names of the civilian victims are read out.

The emotion is always intense as well-trained small schoolchildren sing the *Marseillaise*, and follow it with the British National anthem for the British veterans and survivors of the liberation, who attend the moving bi-lingual service. Generous hospitality is offered by citizens who were unborn in 1944. On the fiftieth anniversary of the Liberation, Brittany Ferries - a "hard headed" commercial company - gave every veteran who crossed the Channel in their ships, a commemorative litre bottle of Calvados! Every shop-window in Normandy was beflagged with flags of Britain, Canada, France and America.

In the first week of August, 1944, Captain David Jamieson of our 7th Royal Norfolks had won a V.C. just across the Orne, in the Forèt de Grimbosq by repelling determined and repeated attacks by crack battle groups of infantry and tanks of 12th SS Panzer Division, by the simple but effective method of directing the fire of our own twenty-five pounders onto his own precarious infantry company positions. Meanwhile I was getting a new engine.

I took the order to 'keep well out of the way and report in the morning', literally, and wandered off for the day into the forested area over the Orne, not far from the scene of the recent battle. In view of the dreaded "S" mines - which, when triggered, jump up in

This one didn't go off

the air to a more 'effective' height before exploding a load of lethal bullets in all directions - I kept a sharp lookout for tell-tale signs. But there was nothing visible.

Eventually I came on a grassy forest track. There were no signs of recent military traffic but as I rounded a corner there were three dead Germans lying on the grass in front of me. They must have had a sudden alarm, and had quickly tumbled out of the forest shack in which they had slept overnight, or even longer, and met their fate by a short and accurate burst of fire.

I went curiously, into the shack.Very carefully indeed, because of the ever-present danger of booby traps. A very cautious inspection revealed that, in fact, they had lived there for some days. It had been a comfortable billet. On the table was evidence of their last meal. They had been enjoying something from home. Half a loaf of black bread, or maybe it was home-made cake, which had been partially unwrapped from some sort of silver paper, was still on the table. An opened magazine was lying beside it. It was the most recent copy of "*Die Stürm*" the official organ of their unit, the Waffen SS. The frontispiece of the shiny magazine showed a composite photo of a heroic-looking SS man wielding a lassoo. Into the large noose of the lassoo had been inserted photographs of about a dozen Jews, Gipsies, and others considered to be sub-species of the human race, detested by the Nazis. "We are clearing the human rubbish from all Europe!" proclaimed the caption.

I put the magazine in my pocket and left the little shack thoughtfully and had another look at the dead SS men. They were virtually unmarked. But these tough young men *had* known exactly what they were fighting for. Now nobody would be able to convince me otherwise. Ahead of us in the coming months, we would see the subjects of this 'lassooing'; the newly released inmates of the concentration camps, shivering a little in their striped uniforms, little better than thin pyjamas, or lying dead in heaps like so much detritus.

Next morning the work on the truck was completed and I drove back to my unit. Another infantry division, the 'Tyne & Tees', had passed through our own depleted divisional areas in pursuit of the

now fleeing Germans, who were desperately trying to escape being left behind in the enormous trap of the Falaise Pocket. But we would take no part in this. Our infantry had been so decimated in eight weeks that the division was to be disbanded. The artillery regiments would form an Army Group of the Royal Artillery, to be sent wherever extra fire-power was required. The Typhoons were now doing the slaughter. Ten thousand Germans had to be buried. There were now well over fifty thousand prisoners. Our artillery regiments were to reorganise for a week or ten days, at Louviers, almost on the Seine. So we drove through the rubble which composed the streets, and most of the houses of Thury Harcourt. I paused for a moment at the 1914-1918 War Memorial. Somebody had placed a Teller mine leaning against the first war's heavy shells, which even more incongruously formed supports for the surrounding chain. Then on past the statue of William the Conqueror in the main street of Falaise and then for miles and miles in more open country, through the awe-inspiring evidence of the slaughter that had been wreaked by the Typhoons. Every hedge or wood, where the fleeing enemy had sought to hide from that aerial vengeance, had its lines of burnt-out tanks and unburied German troops and horses.

The ten days at Louviers - while the debacle of the 'Bridge Too Far' - at the very end of Allied resources was taking place - gave us a view of provincial French life. R.H.Q.was at Le Mesnil Jourdain just a few miles outside the little town, and this gave the R.S.M.the opportunity of instigating a smartening-up programme. A few bits of marching drills were deemed to be appropriate. But I had anticipated him a little by finding a source of pure filtered and chlorinated water in the town itself, where we could fill-up in about three minutes, thus giving us some leeway for our own purposes. Long enough to avoid the marching drills.

We 'filled up' for the first time at the bakery and I drove to a tree-lined square, the Place de la Republic, where I parked the truck under the shade of a tree, and switched off. "What's up?" said Jack somewhat puzzled. "Were not going back there to the farm, to do marching drill" I said, "we'll just sit here for an hour or so: if we go straight back, we'll be roped in every day for all that bull."

So we sat under the tree, and in a few moments a small group of young girls gathered. One of about thirteen, spoke to us in surprisingly good English. She said "Would you like my mother to do your laundry, or help in any way?" This was actually a very welcome offer for there hadn't been much laundry done in the past few weeks. But we took some tins of pilchards over to the middle aged ladies sitting on chairs outside their doors, and we were instant 'heroes'.

The mother was Madame Chalopin, a widow with two daughters, Paulette, and Francoise whom we had already met. Next day we were able to provide them with a few needles, of all things, for they were virtually unobtainable in France for most of the occupation. Coffee, from my mother's first parcel was greeted with cries of delight, and the promise of some rice next day almost brought tears to their collective eyes.

The adjutant came along just after we had had our evening meal. "Could you spare a minute, Sir?" I said. He nodded, and I took him over to the "Swill Hole". It looked as if more than half the pilchards had just been jettisoned into the hole. When we moved on of course the hole would be filled-in. Standard practice. "Well, Kidd. What do want to show me?" In reply I suggested that if he would instruct the Cook-Sergeant to let me have a case of Pilchards, from time to time, I would see if I could swap it for some fresh local produce.

The Cook-Sergeant was none too keen to see his supplies thus depleted but grudgingly let me have a case of pilchards, (or it may have actually been sardines!) One forgets. With this as our start-up capital Jack and I were in business. When we had filled up the tank, we went to swap sardines.Or pilchards. We returned to base in about an hour with almost a hundredweight of new potatoes, and four fat capons which the adjutant bagged for the "mess".

These activities brought a welcome change of diet to R.H.Q. personnel, mushrooms, tomatoes, eggs, ducks and chickens were the order of the day. Even huge amounts of butter; for the local farmers were unable to get their milk away to Paris, and perforce turned the cream into butter. This little enterprise left us with some convertible assets in the form of eight or nine large seven-pound tins of margarine, sensibly stowed away out of sight in our camouflage nets, as insurance for a hungry winter.We used it for making chips until December.

At the Chalopin household the rice was duly made into an exquisite cake which we were asked to share. For a week, we were almost members of the enlarged family, for various friends and relatives kept turning up to share in the pet liberators. We were fully aware that it had been others who had achieved the liberation, and that most of them were now dead, but there was nothing we could now do about it. Our washing was done beautifully, and my French improved considerably. And Paulette was making eyes at me. I was even asked to spend a week-end leave if I managed to get one from Germany, where we were now heading.

But in a few days we set off for Holland. We made Brussels the second day and the population still hadn't stopped waving. Then northwards, into Holland, on past the crashed gliders and other debris of the airborne attacks that were to have struck a decisive blow at Arnhem. Our immediate task was to give artillery support to the 101st U.S Airborne Division just over the bridge at Nijmegen. The bridge was shelled several times a day and there could be no guarantee that we wouldn't coincide our four daily crossings for water supplies in Nijmegan with one of these stonks. A sign on the middle of the bridge said 'You are halfway over! Go like Hell!'

The daily needs of all the invading forces we were still being met, with difficulty, by convoys which had to go all the way back to the Normandy beaches for supplies. This was because the enemy still clung tenaciously to the south bank of the Schelde, to deny us the use of Antwerp's normally excellent port facilities. Thus we were to to give artillery support to the 3rd Canadian Infantry Division in their unenviable task of clearing the Schelde Pocket. The flat land had been flooded and the attacks had to be confined to the long straight roads, all on embankments. At the end of the 'straight bits', was the inevitable 88mm Ack Ack gun firing on fixed lines down maybe two miles of straight road. To support the infantry attacks our guns would be firing 'gunfire'. Twenty four guns dropping "HE", and "Smoke" at this one target, was designed 'to keep enemy heads down' while the attack took place. It didn't always succeed in its objective.

After this clearing was achieved, there was only one thing to stop the immediate use of Antwerp's port facilities, and that was the heavily defended island of Walcheren. It was said that while the attack was being made across the narrow stretch of water, there was 'gunfire' from three artillery regiments. Over seventy twenty-five pounders firing incessantly for half an hour on one small target, the enemy H.Q. the Hotel Brittania.

Next we were moved to support the 15th Scottish division on the west bank of the Maas. This was to be the biggest artillery barrage since the one at Alamein two years before. The big attack was to follow.

It was to remove a deep German salient in our lines. When somebody pressed the start button for the barrage I happened to be driving past a row of neat cornstacks, when every "stack" opened fire with the thunderous roar of heavy artillery. It was like Armageddon.

Colonel Grant had conceived the brilliant idea of having a Regimental Association, knowing that most bods were possessed of, in some cases, fairly large amounts of money. This currency was mostly francs, both French and Belgian, and Dutch guilders. Most non-smokers like myself, had exchanged our weekly cigarette ration, and a duty-free allowance of cigarettes, for hard cash. We hadn't drawn our measly two shillings a day, for weeks. But this 'funny money' couldn't be sent home. Our wallets were full of it.

But there are always ways and means and many took advantage of a scheme to send "flowers for your loved ones" which were paid for in francs or guilders and sometimes the recipient could, with luck and a persuasive manner, exchange the vouchers for real money.

So when it was anounced that foreign currency would be accepted for life-membershp of the new association, virtually all the regiment joined the new association which was thus provided with enough assets to last for almost fifty years.

The second in command, whom I was driving that day, was attending a 'conference' in the middle of a battered little town and in the midst of all the roar of gunfire, a small party of civilians wound their way past the heaps of rubble. One man was carrying a tiny white coffin. It was an intensely sad, baby's funeral procession. As one man, all military personnel present immediately stood firmly to attention and officers saluted. As the funeral party went out of sight, there passed a Military Police jeep. On the back seat, were stood a large number of wooden crosses. 'Ready for the days' dead', I thought, grimly.

But there were few dead that day for the Germans had made a spectacular and efficient retreat during the night. It was a classic. The guns had been firing on empty positions! Colonel Grant called for a jeep and Calderbank drove him on a personal recce, to see just how far the enemy had actually retreated. Calderbank skirted carefully round where he suspected that there may be hidden mines. This went on for about a mile or two but finally there was sustained and heavy enemy fire.

Armed with this useful information about the present location of the enemy, Calderbank was ordered to turn back. But on the way back the jeep did strike a mine. Colonel Grant was severely wounded and died of his wounds a few hours later. Calderbank escaped with severe lacerations but survived.

Next day, as we were 'out of action', about a hundred of us from his regiment solemly witnessed the Colonel's blanket-covered body laid to rest in a temporary cemetery. The 'old man' as we called him had been thirty five. By now it was autumn, and getting cold at nights. Our individual slit-trenches filled up with about a foot of water in a day, so one made one's own arrangements to counter this problem. I had also devised what might well have been the only hot water bottle in the army.

Every night I poured about an egg-cupful of petrol on to an old fire-brick and - standing well back - threw a match at it. When the ensuing flames finally subsided, and the heat of the brick diminished satisfactorily to a safe point, I had only to wrap the still extremely hot brick with newspapers, well tied, and I had a 'hot water bottle' which would still be hot next frosty morning. Perhaps I had invented the storage heater!

A few days later, the Acting Colonel announced to a stunned regiment that the 'Hundred and Tenth' was to be disbanded, and that most of us would be sent to England for retraining as infantry. We would all be needed for the battles still ahead.

Chapter 14
The Greater Felon

The law doth punish man or woman
Who steals the goose from off the common
But lets the greater felon loose
Who steals the common from the goose.
anon.

One of the many assets of our village is our beautiful stretch of the River Eden as it flows northwards towards the Solway Firth from its source in North Yorkshire. But the village fishing rights happened entirely by chance. Somehow these rights had been overlooked, otherwise they would almost undoubtedly have been incorporated into someones' estate. There was plenty of jiggery-pokery at the time of the Enclosure Acts in the first half of the nineteenth century when many of our present day field boundaries were created. And it didn't stop then. Some of the main effects were to consolidate and enlarge the estates of the rich and powerful. Even a few of the Commissioners were capable of being less than scrupulous. There is a field near here which is still called the "Whisky Field", simply because one of the contenders at the time of the hearing had the foresight to slip the Commisioner a few bottles of whisky just before the hearing!

Salmon don't dally very long in the village stretch of water on their way up from the sea to spawn in the river's headwaters. They don't feel secure in comparatively shallow waters. But under the main arch of our lovely old sandstone bridge there is a pool at least twenty feet deep. One can stand on the bridge and see salmon resting; sometimes for a day or two.

Eventually Fred persuaded me to have a go at them. I could use his rod: a former tank aerial, bought for a few shillings from the Army and Navy Stores. Fred had added the fittings which guide the line from the reel, and had achieved an almost professional look. I called at the Post Office to buy an Eden Fishery Board licence and started casting, as Fred had advised,"across and upstream", and then commenced a steady reeling-in of the artificial minnow, which he had recommended for this early stage of the season. A three inch "yellow belly." It doesn't resemble in the slightest, as far as anyone knows, anything on which the salmon has been feeding during its sojourn out in the Atlantic. Salmon, back in fresh water, aren't actually hungry; they never eat again until they return to the sea after spawning. There is a profound biological change in their metabolism. They *can't* eat. This is why they aren't easy to catch! It is thought that they simply bite at an artificial fly or minnow from a feeling of frustration. But nobody knows.

To my astonishment I felt a hefty tug on the line as the lure crossed the deep pool. The violent pull was too strong and determined, to be a trout and immediately I was too excited to remember all that I had been told. Not quite all, however, for I was able to slacken the 'clutch' on the reel so that a sudden rush by the salmon didn't put the nylon line under an impossible strain, but allowed the fish to rush off almost to the far bank, even if I was still apparently reeling him in. Then I had to "work" him back towards me, and try, at all cost, to prevent him rushing through the arch of the bridge. The ten-pound breaking strain line would have been broken in a moment.

Gradually, over probably twenty minutes or so, I began to feel that I was in with a chance, and eventually assumed mastery of the fish, so that I could bring him near enough to be able to steer the noose of my salmon-tailer round the stub of his tail. I could already see the curved hook of his bottom jaw, indicating that it was a cock fish. A sharp pull on the tailer closed the noose and he was mine! Possibly. All I had to do was to reach down and get a firm grip round the base of the tail, and hoist him out onto dry land.

As I moved the fish a yard or two from the bank I felt that I had had a privilege afforded to only a few. I had fished for trout since I was ten, but this was something very different. Quite marvellous. I reached for Fred's 'priest' - a short weighted stick - and was about to adminster the *coup de grâce*, when I became aware of a burly figure behind me. It was one of the adjacent riparian owners, and he was livid. "You can bloody well see its a kelt!" he shouted angrily, "Don't kill it!" But at this moment the salmon gave a powerful heave and slipped down the bank into the water and was gone. The newcomer was a long-standing member of the Eden Fishery Board, I knew. Had been for years. This was sacrilege, he said angrily. Rape, murder, and a large number of other serious offences suddenly paled into insignificance compared with killing a kelt. The Riot Act was comprehensively read.

Of course I agreed with him. That was the worst part. He was right! If it *was* a kelt. But I still have my doubts about that fish, and always will, especially after - in my subsequent fishing career - having returned several dozen unmistakable kelts to the water. But how could I argue against a man reputed to have caught over a thousand salmon in his time? I had to plead ignorance. It was my very first salmon, I said, caught on my very first cast! In fact, I continued, I hadn't had a salmon licence more than half an hour! Eventually he stalked off, still furious and got back in his Land Rover and drove away. I went home thoroughly deflated.

There is something fascinating about the way a salmon starts its life in the highly oxygenated headwaters of the river, where the hen fish lays its eggs in the shallow gravel. The cock fish fertilizes the eggs with a spray of milt, and the eggs are covered with gravel by strong sweeps of the hen's tail.

For every thousand eggs, probably not more than a handful will survive the next few weeks, but eventually a few salmon smolts, the size of minnows, will somehow manage to grow for over a year in the river, before they are drawn irresistibly to the sea. There they will spend at least a further twelve months - some say eating their fill from the rich diet provided by the warm waters of the Gulf Stream off Iceland. Some of them will return to the rivers of their birth after only a year, weighing from five to seven pounds or so as "Grilse", but others - destined to weigh from eighteen to maybe thirty pounds or so when they return to 'their' own river - spend several years in the sea before they return. So on that basis my fish would be about five years old. Later I learned that while many hen salmon succeed in regaining the sea after the spawning, very few cock fish do so. So this fish would probably not have survived anyway.

It was about a month later that I received the letter from the Eden Fishery Board. Their secretary, a Carlisle solicitor, said that the Board had considered my serious offence. He implied that they had had a special meeting about it. They had checked the circumstances,and had confirmed the timing of the issue of my licence. However as a result of these deliberations, and subject to no further infringement of the regulations the Board had reluctantly decided to take no action.

I replied in similar vein. I apologised profusely, reiterating the details of the purchase and timing of my licence, and concluded that "as a result of this most unfortunate incident", I was now not only able to distinguish a kelt - an 'unclean' fish - from a 'clean' salmon, but was also in a position to distinguish a gentleman from a member of the River Board'. There was no reply.

My accuser had been made titular president of our swimming pool committee,started by the local schoolmaster, who acted as secretary, while I was chairman. It had been thought that he might like to be be able to emulate the generosity, say, of the first incumbent of the mansion to whom the village owed its school, the church, and many other acts of generosity. He attended our meetings, taking voluminous notes in his incredibly small hand. A J.C.B. excavated the enormous hole, which was lined with concrete, changing rooms were built, and when eventually came the opening day, it seemed that the 'President' was the obvious choice as the official opener. The press attended in force. One of the tabloid press filled half a page with photographs of him and the Bathing Beauties.

He made the speech of his life, short, witty, and to the point and concluded with an undertaking to give financial help to the next project which was to be that of installing some system for heating the pool. This was likely to be expensive and so his remark received loud applause. But when he added "Especially as I haven't contributed anything so far", nobody believed him. 'He was just being modest", they thought, and there was more warm applause.

By the time, a year or two later, when the fearfully expensive heating equipment was finally to be ordered, he had dropped off the Committee. So a tactfully worded letter was sent recalling his undertaking at the Opening Day, and suggesting gently that it would be an enormous help to the committee if he could let them know to what extent this generosity would amount. The reply tersely stated that unfortunately his circumstances had changed and he wouldn't be able to promise anything. There wasn't a vote, but the illustrious name was quietly dropped from the letter headings.

Fifteen or twenty years earlier in his capacity of Parish Council Chairman, he had been secretly closeted with its Clerk. What they were engaged on was nothing less than a conspiracy. They both could have been jailed. But by the time the foul deed came to light, forty odd years later, the two of them had long been laid to rest.

The Parish Council Clerk had held that position for a number of years. She was sometimes heard to say that her 'father was in the Guards'. This didn't cut much ice with those who knew he was a railway guard. The old minute books naturally don't record the secret meeting between the two, but it undoubtedly occurred although there is no record whatsoever that this important matter was put ever put before the Council.

The County Council had written to all Parish Councils for their help in compiling the Definitive Map. This would henceforth be the ultimate arbiter in all matters relating to footpaths. The Clerk didn't actually record the arrival of this enquiry, but on the response depended the way in which the County Council would determine the very existence, or otherwise of all Public Footpaths in the Parish. If a path was deemed to exist, then it would be shown on the 'Definitive Map', and on the attached Definitive

List. There would then follow what was called a "period of Public Consultation", before the paths would be fixed for all time. But there was to be no such consultation period here. There is naturally no record of the private deliberations with the Clerk. They don't appear in any minute book. The Parish Council itself was kept in total ignorance about the new Definitive Map. (I was a member myself by this time!) We hadn't even seen the old map! If there ever had been one. But, curiously, somehow these secret meetings resulted in the elimination of *twenty three* footpaths from the definitive map! Still there was no public consultation. You have guessed it! Yes, by a curious coincidence most of the deleted paths happened to be on the chairman's estate! This must have appeared on reflection, to the conspirators themselves, as being perhaps a little bit over the top, for it only left six paths in the entire parish! So they *added* a few which had never been public footpaths! Possibly in an attempt to redress the balance One was a farmers 'accomodation lane', which had never been a path. Another led to a now unidentifiable point in the middle of a field where Hannah Wharton had once kept about fifty hens. It followed that she had to go and feed them and gather the eggs daily. So the route Hannah took was entered as a Footpath. The henhouse is long ago blown away, and no one knows the exact place where it stood, so that they are unable erect an "End of Path" sign.

But another of the 'new' paths; after nearly fifty years had passed, caused long, extremely distressing, and fearfully expensive consequences, especially to one old lady who was told that - according to the Definitive Map - the 'path' passed right through the middle of her house! The new Definitive Map simply ignored the fact that the house had no back door!

Meanwhile, all of the paths closed by the conspirators remain deleted, and gone for ever! The Ramblers Association which had at first written to the District Council that they "had no objection to the path being deleted from the Definitive Map", then became formal objectors to the official closing of the path, at a Public Inquiry! Another formal objector was a strangely named organisation; for The Open Spaces Society left an open space on the seat which had been reserved for them.They didn't even bother to turn-up! It took more than three years of effort, at all levels of Local Government, and culminating in the Public Inquiry before the 'path' was finally deleted from the map. But how many thousands more; closed by means which wouldn't stand investigation, are lost and gone forever?

Chapter 15

The Magical Glebe

Because of his magnificent white moustache, with which he could easily have passed for a Battle of Britain pilot, and his name, which had a certain ring to it, few would have taken Tom Entwhistle for a successful poacher. His general reputation locally however, was more than a little suspect. Old Molly Hall who knew everybody's pedigree for miles around, was scathing. "That family's allus bin t'seame. Nowt was ower heavy for them!" Maybe it was this reputation which triggered an old Colonel to challenge Tom as he was spotted crossing the little meadow behind what the Colonel always called his 'small property'.

Years before, my father had been going up to the farm buildings to let out the old sheepdog, but as he passed the tool-shed he thought he heard an odd sort of noise coming from within. As he cautiously opened the door to investigate, Entwhistle came out and without any hesitation asked anxiously, as he scanned the skies, "Hes it faired up yet?" Now he was to display the same quick thinking as when he had peered into next door neighbour's garden at her apple tree, absolutely weighed down with fruit. "Them's good apples!" he said, wistfully, and then added hastily "so they tell me!"

"Stop right there!" had shouted the old colonel, as he loosed-off a shot from his twelve-bore into the air. In reality it was all perfectly safe but in later years the old poacher swore that the pellets had whistled past his head and missed him only by inches. "What's up wid thee?" Tom said, as he halted smartly. And then he added, with a show of indignation, "Thou knows that Ah's on a public footpath! Thou nearly kilt me!"

"Public footpath? Public footpath my grandmother!" snorted the indignant Colonel, "Where the Hell's a Public footpath supposed to go? I've never heard such rubbish! And my gun was actually aiming for the sky! Now; where's this footpath, eh?"

"It gas swinway across this field, an gas ower t'railway in yon corner" Tom asserted, confidently pointing in that direction. "You mean 'diagonally across this field'," said the Colonel somewhat pedantically "and *then* where, for Heaven's sake? Tell me exactly where it's supposed to go then!" "Reet down abacka your hoose to t'river to where t'old mill race used t'gan; reet ower t'tother side" affirmed Tom, stoutly. "Aha!" cried the old fellow, triumphantly."And *then* where does it go, I pray?" "Well, you used t'could cross t'river on't auld steanes n'rocks t'tuther side like ah said!" Tom felt that he was running out of options."Indeed? And *then* where precisely, may I ask?" said the Colonel even more sarcastically. He knew he had his man trapped, for the nearest village in that general direction was at least twelve miles away. Tom hesitated only for a split second, and then replied with absolute conviction."Blencarn smiddy!".

The Glebe itself was like a little island of primeval Britain which somehow had been left - virtually untouched by man - since the creation. It consisted of about seven acres of ancient woodland and what is now always referred to as "wetland". On the Ordnance Survey Maps the word "Issues" appears several times. This means, of course,that the place is absolutely running in water. One can feel the peaty ground shaking under one's feet. A field nearby is called "Swallowholes", and it is well named, for it describes the feeling one gets perfectly. The grass feels as if it is growing on jelly. A post can be driven down almost out of sight with only two or three slight blows of the mallet. There seems to be absolutely no 'bottom' to it.

The seven acres were a totally unimportant part - from an agricultural point of view, that is - of a large farm owned by a sheep farmer who had returned from Australia to retire to his native village but who eventually decided to move to Surbiton,"to be nearer the children" as he said, and so the farm was sold.

"What does t'suppose they larn them at colleges, nooadays?" said one village elder, amazed at the sight of a strange young man running about wildly, rounding-up his sheep, for he absolutely refused to even consider buying a sheepdog."Sec a fella!" said another when he heard of a reported accident with the tin of pilchards in tomato sauce, which had been placed, unopened, on the Aga, to warm up, while he finished his chores. The resulting explosion did little harm except to decorate walls and ceilings with the evenly distributed contents of the tin. No one was hurt, fortunately, and he managed to find something else for his supper.

Then the week-old turkeys started to die. Every day more were lost, and finally he asked a neighbour's advice. As the neighbour said later, "Hoo could you tell a reet clever chap that because of t'bad lighting in't auld building, his turkeys couldn't even see t'watter fountains? They were simply dying uv thirst!" Then the farm was put on the market again and for over twenty years I and everyone else assumed that the "Glebe"- almost in the middle of the land, had been bought too. But I was quite wrong. The old sheep farmer had kept it out of the sale, "in case he ever wanted to go up to Cumberland for an hour or two's shooting".

Nevertheless, as the years passed, and various unidentified livestock picked their way very carefully among the woods, and as sundry anonymous beaters regularly flushed out the pheasants, it was tacitly and naturally assumed locally that the ownership of the small area had been transfered to a new owner although nobody seemed sure.

However, by one of life's extraordinary chances, I met the former farm tenant whom I had known since boyhood, as I walked from Hans Crescent into Brompton Road from a meeting at the Potato Marketing Board's offices. His Aunt - then our village District Nurse - had brought me into the world. When Frank spent his school holidays at my sister's farm he spent hours commiserating with me when I was periodically confined to my bed with severe bronchial asthma. Somewhere about the house is the very bed-table from those days, still bearing the small holes we inflicted in it by using the bed-table as a target for his smuggled 'point two-two' air rifle. The worst damage was concealed, for a time, by plugging the holes with 'Plasticine'.

Frank had once accidentally shot one of these air-gun pellets into my hand. So we had gone up into what my mother called her 'tennis-pavilion', with a razor blade and a bottle of 'Iodene'. I had seen movies of cowboys cutting a cross in the flesh, before 'removing a bullet'. It seemed the logical thing to do. But Frank had turned pale when I asked him to 'cut the cross', and finally had refused outright to take part in the operation. We had no option but to go, still secretly, to the current District Nurse. She would soon manage it! But alas, there was a little note on her door. She was on holiday and the note advised that her deputy would be pleased to help.

This was news of the worst sort, for Annie was the daughter of the local Police Sergeant. We had finally gone round to the Police Station filled with foreboding. Our fears had been realised when we saw the burly figure of Sergeant Coulston washing his car in the drive, but we managed to get past him with some trivial excuse. Annie had finally extracted the pellet with a pair of small tweezers, but all was not well when the Sergeant came into the room and the truth had to come out. We left the inquisition sadder and probably wiser boys. But I kept the pellet, with its small scars and scratches, where Annie's tweezers had slipped several times, still visible, for some years, as a memento!

So Frank and I had coffee together in Harrods and talked. Eventually the talk was of home. He enquired what had become of the Glebe now that the retired sheep-farmer had passed away. "Surely,"I said, "it would have been included in the sale of the farm when it had been sold, twenty odd years before?" But not so; it had never been sold by the old chap! It had been excluded from the sale. Frank had the old sale papers at home. He was quite adamant about it.

It all fell into place. In a few seconds my wrong assumption about the ownership was cleared up. And by one of those amazing tricks of memory, which happen but rarely, my friend could even recall the name of his old landlord's daughter, and that she lived 'somewhere in Greater London'. It only took a few minutes to find her address in the telephone directory and the first stage was set for the eventual purchase of the Glebe.

Negotiations had to be conducted in a very circumspect way indeed, as the slightest hint that an offer to buy was on the cards, would most certainly alert any opposition. In the whole valley it was a pearl almost beyond price from a shooting man's point of view. For within a radius of just over two miles were no less than six commercial shooting estates, rearing a total of maybe six or seven thousand pheasants a year and inevitably a proportion of these reared pheasants wandered away, mostly on foot, from their 'owners' properties and found their way to the Glebe and obviously decided to stay. Somehow the swamps and dark wet woods might have roused some inherited memory of the Asian forests of their ancestors.

The ethics of rearing pheasants and then shooting them,seem almost incomprehensible to the urban population, but game shooting is a very important part of the rural economy. And on the face of it, if there is a distinction between rearing birds and then shooting them, and rearing chickens intensively, and then eating them, the pheasants have the best of it. By miles!

Not being a native British bird, the ornamental Asiatic Pheasant which graces our countryside, would soon be virtually extinct here, but for one thing; artificial rearing. There may be a more stupid bird than the pheasant, but I don't know of it. Many times I have seen hen pheasants, which had had the luck to survive the previous shooting season, with a newly hatched brood of up to a dozen chicks. They might not all be from her own eggs, for the few nests that are made may sometimes be a the collective nest of two or three pheasant hens. Almost all of these chicks will probably be lost within a few days by sheer rank stupidity. A hen will lead newly hatched chicks through streams without even realizing that half her brood have drowned. Then she will return and drown the other half. So there is no real alternative to artificially rearing the vast majority of pheasants in the same way as domestic poultry.

There is an enormous amount of money spent on pheasants. The old adage used to be "Up flies ten-bob, bang goes sixpence, and down falls half a crown!". One can easily multiply those figures by ten now, but the principle is the same. Up flies say,'five pounds', that is the cost of rearing one bird to maturity, after maybe buying it as a 'day-old'; for about two pounds. Then there's the cost of the cartridges, including 'misses', and the end product of all this falls down and is immediately worth about £2.50! And sometimes at the end of the shooting season one can to buy a brace of them in the game merchants shop for as little as £3.50.

But of course, money does come in as well. To participate in a good shoot, with plenty of pheasants driven out of their coverts, hopefully to fly high and fast over the row of guns in a quite modest shoot can cost well over £250 a day. And quite often twice that. But, naturally, that does include lunch!

One of the big problems is that pheasants would rather walk than fly. It is probably quite true to say that many pheasants will be having almost their first flight when they are driven from the coverts to take their chance over the guns. When, years ago, I kept that favourite old breed of domestic hens, the Ancona, I always felt that *they* would have made a much more sporting bird than the pheasant. They could fly faster, higher and further than the average pheasant.

To overcome the quite natural reluctance of pheasants to provide a sporting high-flying target, even the landscape itself has been adapted. And fortuitously, very greatly improved! For generations, woods have been planted on strategic hills, with others just a short flight away. Sometimes a row or two of tall poplars is planted in the lower lying land below to keep the birds flying at the optimum height.

My brother Harold was once tackled by one of his adjacent landowners for shooting pheasants which the latter considered his own property; even when they were not on his own land. "You know Harold," he said, across the hedge, "These are pheasants I have **reared**!" Harold picked up the bird he had dropped, and replied "Aye, them's t'yans I like to shoot, man, they dunt flee so fast" Relations between them were strained for years.

If any of these chaps within a radius of, say, two miles had had the slightest inkling that this choice little property in the centre of the valley was the subject of negotiations to buy, it would have been so easy - they realized too late - for any of them to have simply claimed it by "Adverse Possession", or "Squatter's Rights". The law is quite clear on this. Anyone could have had it without paying a penny. If only, during the preceding twelve years - not twenty-two years, which is sometimes quoted - anybody who had, say, simply repaired or renewed the fences, or done something tangible like that, they could have claimed the Glebe for nothing.

The old boundary fences hadn't actually been repaired or had any maintenance whatsoever, for over eighty or maybe even a hundred years, and it was beginning to show. In some places the 'fences' had virtually disintegrated. So some visible sign of ownership could have been done extremely simply. It would have cost practically nothing. Well, maybe a couple of hundred pounds!

I forced myself to be patient, for it was no good appearing to be anxious. Eventually there was a telephone call from Finsbury Park. "What would I offer, if they *did* decide to sell?" They had considered their options. These really boiled down to selling the Glebe to me, or almost certainly losing the land altogether. I took a deep breath and doubled the figure that I had first thought of. I might just as well be hanged for a sheep as for a lamb, I thought. There would never be another chance. At this moment the property couldn't be offered to any of the other adjacent landowners for they would probably claim it outright! But delay would be risky. If the dark secret leaked out, anybody could claim that some work had been done which would tend to greatly substantiate their claim to ownership. And they could even do some work - surreptitiously, as it were - with oldish fencing posts, to look as if they had been there for years, in support of the claim! It would have been so easy! So the negotiations just had to be kept completely in the dark. They had to be "Most Secret".

The unknown lady from Fisbury Park rang back in ten minutes and accepted the offer. Could they give me the name and address of their solicitor, I asked. Oddly enough, he turned out to be a member of the same local long-established firm of solicitors which had been used by her father. Come to that, as the one her grandfather had used. I was in their office to pay the deposit, only five minutes after it opened next morning. And amazingly, I had the deeds within a fortnight. It had been a close run thing, for one of the firm's partners was reputed to be an old friend of one of the possible contenders. But as it happened *he* was on a fishing holiday in Norway! By the time he returned, it was all over. But it might have easily strained the bounds of confidentiality to the limit!

The following day was the last day of the shooting season, the day when by an admirable tradition, the beaters and helpers who assist on shoots during the season, are asked to have a day's shooting themselves. A nice gesture. Quite often on some of these final shoots there is an edict for this last day, "Cock pheasants only!" This is to in the dubious expectation that it will give any surviving hens an opportunity to breed; for one cock pheasant can gather together a little coterie of several hens. Hope springs eternal. They might, just might, provide next season's birds! I could hear the sound of shots down near the Glebe, as I set off to see my stock, and as I drove the tractor past the new acquisition, I could see one of the 'guns' standing waiting with his twelve-bore right in the middle of *my land* ! What a cheek! I put my own gun on my arm and walked carefully towards him across the quivering bog.

He was a stranger to me, but as I got nearer, I could see the surprise on his face. He couldn't believe what he was seeing. Somebody gate-crashing! But this astonishment increased dramatically as I sharply accused him of poaching. "I'm quite flabbergasted to see anybody poaching on my land!" I said reproachfully. "Didn't you know that this is my field?" "How long has it been *your* field?", he replied angrily. "Since yesterday!" I said, with relish, "You had better tell whoever it is who sent you here, that I'll do all the shooting that is going to be done on this land in future!"

The chap stalked off, and I could hear him muttering as he went, towards the far wood, behind which, I presumed, he would find one of the organisers. I decided to wait on the farm lane and see if there were any repercussions. But there were none.

Neighbourly Relations

I established a relatively neighbourly relationship with a local farm lad. When one of his sheep expired, for example, and needed burying sharpish, I would ring him to tell him the sad news. "It's just over by that tree which was struck by lightning last year down by the long meadow". Although not absolutely overjoyed at the thought of digging a large hole, in hard dry soil, he was aware that he would be in a very precarious position if an unburied carcase was, quite rightly, reported to the Police.

Sometimes, when my tractor got stuck in the bog, Jimmy would bring over his tractor and, with my own strong length of chain - without which I never ventured onto the Glebe - would drag me out, onto firmer land. Sadly, one day the chain slid off the back of my trailer somewhere down the lane and was lost. Jimmy promised to keep his eye open for it. And I knew he would. But it was never found. And naturally his boss never knew of these neighbourly interludes.

Early next season, shooting was to be heard in the vicinity of our new property. I knew that there was every likelihood that the temptation to send beaters through our wood would be almost irresistible, for the adjacent shoots had been doing it for over twenty years. So I drove slowly across the primitive causeway which had been made with enormous effort - and several dozen tractor loads of stones and rubble - which allowed us to drive, ever so carefully across the bog, and tucked the old tractor away out of sight. I parked myself not far from the brand-new boundary fence, and stood in the middle of some tall reeds - much higher than a man - which grew amid the ancient alder trees. I could hear the whistles which were being used to control the beaters, or maybe the dogs, or both, and certain signs indicated that they were coming my way. A covey of partridges flew very rapidly right over the wood, and a few crows which had decided to keep well out of harm's way followed them hurriedly. Then could be heard the sounds of someone possibly helping, possibly throwing, a dog over the new fence which was of the strong square-mesh variety; galvanized, with barbed wire on the top. Came a stifled curse. Whoever it was, he had probably got his trousers torn. 'Shame!' I thought, wryly. If he was intending to come into the wood he would have to jump the beck now, any second. There was a splash, and another fluent curse only a few yards away. He'd probably fallen a bit short. Not one of his best days. A cocker spaniel industriously worked its way right past my feet. It didn't even look up, for it was hugely enjoying itself. There was a quiet whistle to the spaniel and then I could hear footsteps directly approaching me. I kept absolutely still and silent, and in another second someone parted the reeds in front of me! It was Jimmy! No more than a yard from my face. But with a presence of mind to rival that of old Tom Entwhistle, he asked anxiously, "Did you ever find that snigging-chain?"

A few years later I surprised a party of small boys playing Cowboys and Indians in the nearest of the two woods. I was a bit surprised myself and in a way quietly pleased with this apparent defiance of political correctness. But I called them up to me and sternly asked,"Do your mothers know where you are ?" Silently they shook their heads. "Well," I went on, "How do you think that they will know where to start looking for your bodies?" The boys, still silent, shook their heads. "Go on, boys" I said very firmly, "My advice to you is to go off back to the lane. Walk very carefully indeed, and never *never* come back! These bogs will swallow a bullock".

Next we hired a J.C.B. to clean out the biggest water course, and then a smallish 'flight-pond', and so we had our very own duck-flighting. For the uninitiated, a flight-pond is "fed" with small amounts of grain on a fairly regular basis during the winter, and several times during the shooting season we would ensconce ourselves in the camouflaged corrugated-iron "hides", at about twenty minutes before the expected evening flight of mallards, and sometimes teal. Favourable weather for duck-shooting can mean wild gales, rain and or hail. The ducks probably assume that we will have more sense than turn out in such weather. Then there was an abortive effort to establish a reasonably large fishing pond.We had an unlimited amount of the main requirement, water. All we needed was a hole. A big one, which would keep itself continually refilled, and while enhancing the general ambience, could also be stocked with trout. It might even be a commercial success; the human trait is not to grudge the money one spends on pleasure.

The man from the Plant-Hire company had a look and gave a quote to dig the 'hole'. Once it was dug we knew it would fill in no time."No problem", he said. "The site is *extremely* soft", I warned again. But he was absolutely confident and related tales of even bigger holes that they had dug in even wetter sites. Next day a huge transporter arrived with what I learned was a "Hymac" digger. A huge machine on tracks. I wondered if it could actually propel itself along the lane. In fact as it went slowly along it widened the lane by about a foot.

The machine pushed out the telescopic arm which supports the huge 'bucket'. These monsters are fascinating to watch. The driver lowered the enormous bucket and took hold of about fifteen hundredweights of primeval earth - untouched since the Creation.

As the colossal weight began to take effect, the Hy-Mac began to sink. Inexorably it settled down until all one could see was the operator's cab - normally about seven feet high. The tracks had completely vanished into the slime. But with almost unbelievable calm, the white-faced operator tipped out the weighty contents of the bucket, and swung it round a hundred and eighty degrees, before lowering away and taking a huge bite out of the much firmer ground behind before 'pulling' towards safety, and at the same time putting the submerged tracks into a slow reverse.

Ever so slowly the machine emerged from the jaws of death. The procedure with the bucket was repeated many times, until the thing stood on firmer but still shaking ground. The driver was pale but quite surprisingly fluent, and swore that the whole idea was 'bluddy stupid', and drove the machine back to the transporter. I never received a bill. And within six months all trace of the drama had vanished.

The flora interested local botanists. There were at least three different sorts of wild orchids already growing on the causeway. The fauna normally includes about seven roe deer which rarely leave the precincts, for they seldom attempt to jump wire fences unless they are hard pressed; they just move quietly out of sight, as do the red squirrels. The odd fox or badger can be an occasional visitor, and various small fish must come up the beck from the river - although I never see any - for now and again we are lucky enough to see a kingfisher! And there can be a solitary heron. Buzzards,now much more plentiful, wheel around at their optimum height of about ninety feet or so 'mewing' to each other. I live in hopes of seeing a Reed Warbler's nest with the gate-crashing occupant of a young cuckoo. It is a quite magical place.

My old friend Charlie and I arrived one night at the flight-pond. We were too early! It was about twenty minutes before "duck-time". This is what we call the time (according to the light conditions' - not Greenwich mean-time) when the ducks would decide spontaneously to leave the river where they had spent the day, and now would pass the hours of darkness on somebody's duckpond where they are accustomed to find a daily feed of barley. In the nearest of the two woods some pheasants were noisily trying to sort themselves out for bedtime, and my friend suggested that if I stood at a strategic point on the "causeway", he would go round behind the wood and flush a few of them in my direction. And off he went on a circuitous route to drive towards me.

I took up my position on the 'causeway' and waited. And waited. Eventually I heard a warning shout. "Malcolm!" I slipped off the safety catch. But absolutely nothing happened. So once more I slid the safety catch back on and waited. It was getting dark more quickly than we had thought. Long columns of rooks were wheeling about and 'talking' to each other on the way back to their distant roosts. They too seemed to have miscalculated the light conditions. Suddenly there was another urgent shout. "Malcolm!" Again I slipped off the safety catch. But there seemed a desperate note to the voice. I yelled "Are you stuck?" The anxious reply, a mixture of anxiety, irritation and embarassment, came back through the gloom,"Yes!!"Charlie actually sounded quite annoyed. Pulling off my heavy "Swedish Army greatcoat", I unloaded the gun and quickly stowed it away in my battered old four-wheel-drive in the lane, and extracted the tow-rope. Armed with this I set off for the wood. I hailed my friend and instructed him to give a shout, now and again so that I could locate him in the now gathering gloom of the wood.

When I eventually did locate him, he had already sunk up to his waist in one of the "swallow holes" about which I had warned the boys. I threw him an end of the rope, which he tied round what was left of his visible waist and I fastened the other to a small tree; as high as I could reach. Then he was helped to move towards me, aided by branches which I broke off and threw to him. They allowed him to commence the slow process of getting himself out, by heaving one leg out of the mire and then by placing his foot on the branch, which - although it sank under his weight - still enabled him to make some forward progress. Then another branch, and another,until finally he reached firmer ground. It took almost an hour. He says it was longer.

When he rang, a couple of hours later, he seemed more cheerful. He said that he had soaked for nearly an hour in a hot bath where he said "the sludge would scarcely go down the plug-hole!" and after a couple of large whiskys he felt considerably better and knew that he was a very lucky man.

A few weeks later an old Army pal rang asking if he could spend the night and reminisce a little about old times. I hadn't seen him for twenty years. I suggested that if he brought a pair of wellies I would take him duck-shooting. Ron went back all the way to Belle Vue in 1939, but he had actually been commissioned and ended up as a Staff Captain. I hadn't seen him for twenty years. When he was with us 'lower ranks' he had made the mistake of relating how his train home from work in pre-war London was a local one and that the porters announced its departure by hollering "Harpenden Only!" This caught the imagination of us drivers, and as long as Ron was with us he always had this phrase as his nickname!

Ron arrived from his business trip to Dundee, a trifle later than 'duck-time' and the ducks had already dropped in at the pond when we both arrived. They rose noisily and departed and Ron's hopes were dashed. "Never mind!" I said, "If we settle down in the hides one or two might come back!" And in twenty minutes one or two *did* drop swiftly down to resume their interrupted feed. But they had a charmed life; as Ron had never fired anything but a standard Lee-Enfield; and missed every time. But as the last light faded almost entirely, a late-comer dropped swiftly down."There's one, Ron!", I hissed quietly. "Where, where?" he replied. "Left, left!" I said. "Up! Up! FIRE!" And down it came. Ron had never even seen it! One might have thought we had been in an Ack-ack Regiment.

When he wrote to thank us for the hospitality, a few days later, he said how much his family had 'really enjoyed the duck!' Naturally they felt that they had to invite 'the old lady next door', who had dressed the duck for them. But then his sister and family had arrived, and of course *they* had to have a share. Ron concluded his letter by saying how thankful his wife was "to have had a couple of pounds of sausages in the fridge!"

Chapter 16

Redcap!

We had had a very uncomfortable time on the wintry North Yorkshire Moors, with the Green Howards. In essence it was because we hadn't been killed. We even felt a bit guilty ourselves. 'You're not in the bloody artillery now' was heard daily from hard-bitten infantry sergeants who had somehow survived, and most of us were therefore feeling somewhat apprehensive about the immediate future. And that's a very considerable understatement.

Quite seriously, most of us were absolutely sure that we would be dead in about four weeks after we eventually arrived at an Infantry Reinforcement Unit in the eastern Belgium town of Louvain. Although we were feeling somewhat disorientated we still felt, in a way, that we were the 'Hundred and Tenth', as we were still with about three hundred of our old mates. Still some ésprit de corps The only thing was that, having been Green Howards for several weeks, we now overnight had been turned into Cameron Highlanders, with a bob on our berets. But thankfully, no kilts.

Surprisingly, the war suddenly seemed to have entered its last phase. While we were returning from leave, the Rhine had been crossed and we were still alive! It now seemed that we were destined to remain in the Holding Unit for at least several more weeks. One day however, on the unit notice board appeared an appeal for volunteers for Military Police duties in Germany. Ignoring the old Army edict, 'never volunteer', we volunteered virtually as one man, and we were sent as a body to the newly formed Military Police Training School at Tournai, Belgium.

The school was in a large Seminary which had just been requisitioned. On arrival we were divided into squads of thirty and marched away to classrooms. My squad was to start learning elementary German. The tutor was a Belgian civilian,whose opening words were interrupted by the entry of the Commandant, an elderly Major with 'first war' ribbons. It transpired that none of the officers or instructors - middle aged Military Police reservists- who were to be the instructors or staff, could speak French!

"Excuse me Monsieur Hazard, I just want to ask if anybody here speaks French! Anybody?" My hand was the only one raised. This was on the strength of being second from bottom in my class at school. "Could you please try him out, Monsieur?" asked the Commandant. So Monsieur Hazard - fluent in six European languages - tried me with a few simple questions, all of which apparently, I answered reasonably well, for Hazard said, "He's quite good M'sieur". "Right! Come with me!" said the Commandant, "go to the Quartermaster and draw Sergeant's stripes. You will be Permanent Orderly Sergeant as well as being Interpreter. Good luck!" The Commandant himself was no linguist but he was a 'trier'. He had found some difficulty in asking one of the Belgian civilian staff to slip over to the Officer's Mess for his cigarettes. Eventually he formulated the request. 'Major Andrews ici!" he said slowly and clearly, 'Cigarettes, la bas!' The man understood his meaning however and returned in due course with the packet of 'Gold-Flake'.

So I was launched unceremoniously into a new army career. In the main it was being in charge of our Belgian civilian employees. We had a full complement for the kitchens - for all told, the unit was over three hundred and fifty strong - plus, of course the civilian-cooks, kitchen-staff, signwriters, cleaners and so on, and in the workshops, old Charles Brice. A marvellous joiner, he was also the only man who could understand the workings of the boilers. Charles helped me from day one, when I had been given a standard contract for the purchase of, of all things, the swill. A local pig farmer was the prospective purchaser, but not until he had signed the appropriate form. Charles and I sat on a bench in his workshop and translated it into French. We couldn't find the equivalent for 'swill', so 'eatable rubbish' had to do instead.

I didn't know it at the time but apparently a Belgian accent is regarded with mild amusement in Metropolitan France, but I found it quite practical to dispense, say, with 'four twenties' for 'eighty', and use 'octant' instead. 'Four twenties, less ten' seemed inordinately clumsy for 'seventy'! 'Four twenties plus ten' for 'ninety' didn't sound as easy to Belgians as 'nonant'! Or me, for mathematics was never my strong point

It was thought to be helpful if I was present when the local Military Police Unit carried out raids on suspect premises. One such was when they raided a local establishment which comprised a cafe cum brothel cum garage. The workshop end was full of army motor bikes, in various stages of conversion to innocent civilian machines.

I was with their senior officer, another middle aged major, when visiting to an Army Information office, where information on supplies, repairs, and most importantly, fuel, could be obtained by convoys which were still operating the long haul from the Normandy beaches. As we entered the requisitioned shop, a soldier was waiting his turn at the desk. The Major came up behind him and barked "How long have you been a deserter, corporal? "The man came to attention, saluted, and replied "Three months,Sir!" Within seconds he was marched away under arrest. He would certainly have been running some sort of petrol racket with his vehicle. Later I asked what had led the Major to suspect that he was a deserter. "His boots", he replied. "His boots were so worn down at the heels that no self respecting unit would have tolerated it" I never heard what the corporal was charged with, but no doubt it wasn't just 'failure to see that his boots were in good repair.'

Life in Tournai resumed its normal pattern within weeks. Only at the railway station was one reminded of the missing. A small group of civilians met every train from the East in case a loved one returned from forced labour in Germany. There was a rumour that one such had died from a surfeit of unaccustomed rich food.

There was a bit of a culture shock for us British. I had learnt the patois for "Where is the toilet?" But when I used it in a cafe, as a matter of some urgency, "Ou est la cour?" I was directed to the aforesaid yard - fitted with a couple of open air 'stalls' - to find two sweet old ladies a yard or two away, happily knitting in the evening sun. Red faced I did a prompt 'about turn'. "Voulez vous un piss, M'sieur?" asked one old dame, kindly, moving her chair a little to one side for my benefit. "No, Madame, merci!" I replied, red-faced, doing a smart about-turn, "Demain, peut etre." Maybe tommorow!

Life had returned to normal in the streets. Daily deliveries of beer were as much in evidence as milkmen back at home. A delivery man with a horse-drawn dray, halted near the kerb, greeted an elderly lady of his aquaintance at the other side of the road by raising his hat with old-world courtesy, with one hand, while with the other - so to speak - he relieved himself against one of the waggon wheels.

Jimmy called at my office. They've rumbled me! "he said, without rancour; his service record had caught up with him. Especially the glass-house episode, and he was to be returned to the holding unit, together with other more obvious misfits. He eventually ended up in charge of a large number of Wehrmacht horses, learnt to ride well, and developed a lifelong love of horses which, in later years, could only be expressed in a Salford betting shop.

As the first squads passed-out and departed, the school itself moved up into Germany. It wasn't surprising that it was tacitly assumed that I would continue to be the unit interpreter. My whole but my whole vocabulary consisted of 'donner und blitzen'.

We drove over the new Roosevelt pile-bridge over the Rhine, alongside the war-damaged remains of the old one, to Bad Lippspringe - a spa town in the Teutobergervalt - which most exceptionally showed no signs of war damage. My first task was to requisition a number of rooms from some frightened nuns in a convent. Accommodation was at a premium, and most houses in the town were accommodating quite large numbers of bombed-out relatives and evacuees. Monty had decreed that there was to be no fraternisation with German civilians. Naturally this was impossible to enforce. Another order was that no British soldier would have to stand in queues for his meals. They would have to be waited-on. The Town-Major arranged through his German subordinate that twenty or thirty girls would act as waitresses for our unit. The head girl, Inga Seager, spoke quite good English, and told me that her mother, a retired teacher, would doubtless be pleased to give lessons in elementary German. I was accompanied for my first lesson by one of our office staff, Henry, a lance-corporal from a service regiment, who also wanted a few lessons. He had owned a fashionable prep-school near Windsor before the war. Henry was a scholarly figure, who had been called-up late in the war, aged forty. His instructors alleged that he was probably the most unsoldierly looking man in the Army of the Rhine.

We had thought it a good idea to take a few tins of this and that, which we knew would be welcomed, and also a tin of real coffee from home, as we went for our first lesson. All Europe seemed to be thirsting for the first cup of real coffee. After years of erstatz 'coffee', made from acorns, we knew it would be really appreciated, and more than pay for our lessons.

We got a lift in a passing three-tonner right into the little town, and as the higher ranking man I had naturally sat in the cab with the driver. The latter dropped us off just opposite the requisitioned cinema, where a long queue of off-duty soldiers was awaiting the first showing of a Bing Crosby film. As Henry jumped off the back, several tins of bully beef shot like shrapnel from under his battle-dress blouse onto the pavement. For the benefit of the spectators of the little drama, I immediately 'arrested' Henry, scooped up the 'evidence' and marched him off out of sight round the corner to the Seager's flat. Next day rumour had it that at least one black-marketeer was awaiting court-martial.

Soon we were moved into a large barracks complex of the former Werhmacht training area, and received a new intake of reluctant squaddies. Volunteers had now completely dried up, and being stationed even for a few weeks at somewhere resembling Catterick appealed to very few. I was an exception, having the time of my life on the Senne in yet another home-made canoe.

We got a new Commandant, and the time seemed ripe for another change of direction. I asked if I could be an instructor and be given one of the new squads, and the offer was readily accepted. After five years, my military career seemed to be taking off at last. I informed my lads that if any of them failed to pass the exam, at the end of the course, I would recommend that they be allowed to complete another course. This was enough of an incentive for all but one to pass with distinction, with the highest pass rate of all the squads. The only snag for me had been the need to swot-up the next days' subjects every night. The old-sweat sergeant/instructors were really put out and hinted darkly that I was a phoney. But I knew my squad and knew that they had absorbed all that was in the book. They didn't know what awaited them: the sorting out of the human detritus and hordes of 'displaced-persons' from all over Europe. The books had never envisaged circumstances like these. There was no guidance on these points, they would just have to do the best they could.

Several months later, after the week-end leave in Louviers, my demobilisation grew nearer. Although we were more than ready for civvy street, it was strange that as the time grew nearer, many acknowledged that they "maybe wouldn't mind doing a bit longer". A bit like reluctant prisoners being discharged against their will. By now everyone knew their demob 'group', and those who had been twenty one at the outbreak of war were scheduled for demobilisation in January 1946.

After my last leave I felt that there had been enough water under the bridge to allow me to go home, for surely I would have outgrown the old enemy, asthma? It was intensely disappointing however to find that my old enemy recurred, in a big way, within a couple of days. However, as my demob was imminent on the 23rd of January, I felt that there was no option but to return to my unit. I was quite reconciled to leaving the canoe behind, but there was still quite a bit of personal property. I got lifts across three countries - easy for anyone in C.M.P uniform - and arrived back to camp to find my fellow sergeant, Stan Cox, was still on leave. I crawled into bed but sat up all night gasping for breath. I hadn't had asthma as bad as this since I was a schoolboy.

It was even worse in the morning. Even at the risk of a delayed demob, I had to do something for no one even knew that I was there. I determined to attract attention by throwing a boot at the door of our room. It would have to be at the precise moment when someone marched past. At the critical moment however, even though my boot had hit the door fair and square, the anonymous feet went marching on. On reflection, however, I realised that a boot hitting a door doesn't normally create repercussions in a barracks.

It seemed ages before I heard more marching feet: at least two pairs. My other boot hit the door with a thud and the door immediately opened to admit an angry Orderly Officer and his sergeant. He was all for sending for an ambulance but I persuaded him instead to send someone on a motor bike to the nearest Field Dressing Station - as they were still called - with a note explaining the situation, and asking, as a matter of urgency, for half a dozen Ephedrine tablets. Within a short time the rider was back with my life-savers. They really were, and in twenty minutes I was as normal as I would ever be. By that evening I was having a last go in my canoe on the Senne, before giving it away. It was as if it had just been a bad dream. Next day I was sent home.

At the transit camp near the Dutch border we were allotted to huts for the night in bunches of ten. Sergeants and warrant officers were two to a hut. Soon we would all be civvies. I awoke about midnight to find the infantry sergeant next to me was wide awake. "No" he replied to my query. He never slept well, really. So we talked and he told me his story. He had landed early on "D" Day commanding an infantry section. Normally ten or twelve men, a section is the smallest fighting unit in the Army, the part nearest the enemy. That first day it lost three men killed. Two wounded and one missing altogether.

There was reorganisation. Always happening in the infantry, he said. The survivors were amalgamated into quite small sections. He had five new men in time for that attack on Caen. Through the standing corn which gave cover, but no protection from machine-gun bullets. Section reduced to four. Again it was made-up to strength, in time for the six weeks of steady slogging, as the British and Canadian front moved steadily southwards through ideal defensive country; the Bocage, with high hedges on earth banks. "Nothing spectacular", he said, "just steadily losing men."

There was a lull once or twice. This time it was the Germans who were on the receiving end. The Falaise pocket was where the Typhoons were the dogs of war. These ferocious little fighter-bombers had arrived on the scene. Every little wood or coppice; where the Wehrmacht vehicles and men had sought cover from the dreadful vengeance wrought by the Typhoons, was a mass of scrap-iron, already rusting red around the grim charnel houses. By the time the many times much-reinforced section had reached the Reichwald Forest - right on the German border - his entire section had been 'killed, wounded, or missing' three times. He had been the only survivor, three times.

The attack took place with the 'benefit' of a smoke screen. (It might easily have been from my own regiment for that was our. last action as a unit. 'Operation Schwansong'!) Each twenty-five pounder smoke shell contains three smoke canisters, about the size and shape of a half-tin of evaporated milk. The shell itself is set to explode at a given height near the end of its trajectory, and the three canisters splay out and, after hitting the ground, make dense clouds of smoke for several minutes. As the attack hopefully advances, the range is gradually lifted by the forward artillery observation officer, and his signaller, as they move on with the infantry. As the many times reinforced section moved forward the sergeant was absolutely sure that, this time, he would 'cop it'. It stood to reason. Then he was hit. One of the smoke canisters fell a few yards short and hit him full on his back. It might have actually gone through him but he still had his entrenching tool - a very short spade - strapped across his back. "I thought I was dead" he said, " but some of the lads pulled me into a shell-hole and then they went on. I never saw any of them again, I don't know what happened" he said gloomily. "I had four months in hospital and never went back to the battalion". It sounded as if he was suffering from a guilt complex. Just for being alive.

Chapter 17
Short Leave to Louviers

The Chalopins had replied to my Christmas card with a warm invitation to visit Louviers if I could get a short leave from Germany. The war would soon be over! So in that first post-war early summer I had a trip back to France on the somewhat chaotic European railway system. It was a bit like present day British Rail. It took a bit of working out and a fearful amount of patience. They had some excuse, for there had certainly been a lot of disruption; but eventually I arrived at Louviers where there was what amounted to a reception committee. The reception commitee of three awaiting my delayed arrival consisted of Paulette, Françoise and a tall young man, André, who was introduced as 'Paulette's fiancee'. This was a bit of a setback, something I hadn't expected.

But André was a very nice young chap. Gradually I caught up with developments in the family since the previous year. Madame Chalopin, a widow, had married a widower, M. Chapel, who was about to retire from the Police Force in Paris. André was his eldest son, and another son Robert eventually married Françoise. So all three became Mesdames Chapel!

In the first post-war autumn of 1946, I paid a short visit to Paulette and André, now established in the little village school at Gamache en Vexin. In the practical way they do things in France, André taught the elder children and Paulette was in charge of les enfants, to whom I was introduced as a War Hero! Gamache is east of the Seine in the centre of a vast agricultural plain and the Sugar beet harvest was just beginning.

Twenty years later I was, in the early days of my cattle business, and driving my old lorry with a load of ten cows down the A6 to deliver to a customer at Weston Super Mare and had chosen to drive overnight. I had just cleared Shap Fell when I picked up a couple of hitch-hikers who looked about all-in. French boys. This gave me an opportunity to try and revive my French. It appeared that they were from 'near Rouen'. After we had finished discussing Rouen, of course, I asked, "whereabouts exactly, 'near Rouen?'"

Well - it turned out - it wasn't Rouen after all. It was nearer a little town called Étrapagny. I got quite interested at this point for I had once been round the sugar-beet factory, there, I said. I didn't say, however, that this factory was almost new, while the sugar-beet factory at Cupar, Fife - to which I had formerly consigned my own small amount of sugar-beet - had been closed down in some Common-Market deal to 'allow more sugar to be produced in France'. And natually, less in Britain! Then the boys fell asleep and I concentrated on my driving.

There is a fearful amount of rubbish talked about livestock transit, almost exclusively of course, by people who don't know the slightest thing about it. But having personally driven about three thousand dairy cows the length and breadth of the United Kingdom, and despatched more than twenty thousand by commercial livestock hauliers, I can confidently assert that provided they are properly loaded, cows are capable of very long journeys without the slightest ill-effect. The proof of this assertion is provided by the undoubted fact that freshly calved cows can be unloaded after a two or three hundred mile journey, and within a couple of days be yielding their full yield of milk. There is just one proviso, the lorry must keep keep moving. Cows aren't like people standing in a bus, they stand four square. But once the lorry halts for more than a minute or two they become uneasy. It's only natural, they want to get out.

As I write, valuable racehorses worth probably fifty thousand pounds apiece, are being loaded at Greystoke for tomorrow afternoon's big race, two hundred miles away. How much proof is needed?

The boys slept on as I drove through the night with these thoughts.. Then, as I knew that their immediate destination was Portsmouth, from where they were booked on a boat for Le Havre I felt I had to waken them at Bristol. I pulled up and they duly awoke.

The cows started moving about slightly as they always do. I didn't want to prolong the au-revoirs.

But I was still curious about Étrapagny. "I've been to the Sugar Beet factory at Étrapagny", I said, "What is the name of your village?" "Gamache-en-Vexin" "Gamache-en-Vexin!" I said with a sudden recollection,"You must know Monsieur and Madame Chapel?" "They are my parents!" said the boy, "You must be Malcolm Kidd!" We looked at each other silently. It seemed an extremely strange meeting; to say the least. They pulled their rucksacks out, shook hands and thanked me gravely, before they took up their position to, hopefully, get a lift in the general direction of Devizes, Southampton - and next day - Gamaches en Vexin, or wherever it was that they now lived. I decided to wait a little and 'see them off'. A car fortuitously pulled up for them up almost immediately. They bundled their gear inside and climbed in. It was only as the car drove out of sight that I realized that I hadn't obtained their addresses.

Chapter 18

Mail-Order Cows!

It sounds ridiculous but its perfectly true. I became a Mail Order Cattle salesman! I had come to the conclusion that sixty acres simply couldn't provide me with the the standard of living to which I would like to become accustomed. There was an urgent need for diversification and expansion.

I made an initial investment of seven pounds to further this ambition by inserting a small advertisement in the advertising columns of the Farmers Weekly, offering to purchase dairy cows in our renowned North Country marts for farmers who couldn't do it for themselves. Most parts of the country had no long established marts where good *young* cows were offered for sale. And undoubtedly there would be many, like myself, who simply hadn't the capital to expand. So I visited the local branch of an H.P.Company and had a long chat with the manager.

It was a pleasant surprise, for they would be more than willing to provide finance, subject of course, to the credit-worthiness of the individual famer concerned. This would naturally include as standard practice, a reference to the prospective customer's bank, plus, of course, to the company's own mysterious 'black-lists'. Thus I was propelled into the world of finance. My first advert produced only one phone-call. I explained as lucidly as I could the basis on which my business was to be conducted. This had drawn heavily on my own unfortunate experience with the Guernseys from Reading.

I had returned home from the Army, early in 1946 to find that my four Guernsey heifer calves, which I had bought whilst on manouvres on Salisbury Plain three years earlier, and which I had sent by rail to my sister's farm, had all recently calved their first calves. Four of these were heifer calves so I was now the proud owner of a nucleus of a small dairy herd. But there was an urgent need for mature cows producing an economic amount of milk. This meant, in effect, buying some third calved cows which would be at the peak of their productive life.

There wasn't any way in which these Guernseys could be bought north of say, Oxford, so I availed myself of the services of a widely advertised cattle dealer from Reading. He would supply the very cows I wanted. What was more, he would have them delivered within a week of the clearance of my cheque. I had arranged the overdraft with my bank manager who could see the need for the cows. A normal business transaction.

When the cows arrived, I was somewhat uneasy about them, but there wasn't anything really specific about which I could complain. Perhaps they would settle down in due course. After a week or two, however, I was convinced that they were a very moderate lot. And when the milk-recorder came on his routine visit he noticed that all the cows had National Milk Records ear numbers. This enabled him to obtain details of the cows' previous lactations. Apart from showing that their milk yields had been, well, abysmally low, these showed that they were all from one herd and that without exception they had all calved at least *six* calves. They were really bovine old age pensioners.

It meant that their milk production was on a declining curve.I had specifically ordered second and third calvers, cows which would be at the peak of milk production, I asked the National Farmers Union to take up the matter on my behalf. They ascertained that the cows had been bought by the dealer from the home farm of a well known member of the aristocracy. This didn't make my predicament any better, as any redress would have to come from the man who had sold them to me.

Letters flew backwards and forward for months. Counsel's opinion was sought. It emerged that one of the cows had just calved its seventh calf! I was never again to see a cow so old. After a year the dealer made an offer of ten pounds. Not per cow, but in total. This was naturally refused but in the end I got absolutely nothing for by that time the dealer had gone bankrupt. If I had learned what I later did when disputes arose, I would have hired a lorry and returned the cows to the dealer and sued him for the money!

Thus there seemed to be a complete dearth of honest sources from which farmers could buy honest cows and I resolved that I would be the man who could fill this deficiency.

It was the start of a completely new career. I decided to ask cash customers for a fairly nominal sum - say a hundred pounds with the order - and the balance would be paid to the lorry driver on the arrival and approval of the cattle. Nothing could be more fair. And additionally, on the modest deposit cheque would be provided the name and address of the prospective customer's bank, thus enabling me to make an inquiry about the much more vital remaining portion without actually having to *ask* for it!

Bank inquiries, I found, to some surprise, were part of normal business procedures. The reports came back with a man's business 'soundness' revealed in one cryptic sentence. Most bank customers would be furious if they knew that their own bank disclosed their private business to third parties but I was told that it 'happens all the time'. And I would have been bankrupt several times if this facility hadn't been available. The very highest accolade was "Quite undoubted", of which I only ever had one single example.

The most desirable bank report normally, would be "Respectable and trustworthy, and good for the amount". Coming down the scale however, some reports would be qualified. There would be words of caution: "Respectable and trustworthy, but the sum mentioned is larger than normal for this account". This left me in a dilemma, although in many cases the customer might be drawing on funds about which the bank manager knew nothing. Then would be barely concealed warnings, after the usual preamble about being respectable. I didn't care twopence about respectability, if the money was forthcoming. "We can't answer for your figure" meant that caution would have to be the watchword. Often there was still a dilemma. Even a visit to the farm wouldn't prove anything for anyone could borrow a new combine harvester or other costly items for a day or two to stand about and give a false impression.

I knew that there had always been an intense pride in all types of livestock in our border counties, and a regular weekly trade in freshly calved cows had developed with the industrial revolution. Good young cows, originally exclusively Shorthorns, but now with more and more Friesians; cows which were in the prime of life and milk production had been required for the town dairies in Manchester, Liverpool and other large centres of population round about the time of the Industrial Revolution. The cows had to be kept close to where the customers lived as production methods then were not very conducive to good keeping qualities of the milk. Coolers, and fridges were still in the future. So the cows were brought to the customers. They were kept in enormous town cowsheds and milked until their milk dried up, almost a year or even eighteen months or so later, and then they were sent for slaughter almost as prime beef, and many would then realise nearly their original cost price.

It followed that there was a steady demand year in year out for these freshly calved cows, and the main choice was for cows which had just calved their third calf, and were therefore in the peak of production. In the main the trade had been sewn-up by dealers who handled the trade to their own satisfaction. My own experience of getting a load of cattle unseen from a dealer had taught me a very expensive lesson.

My small but carefully worded advertisement in the columns of the *Farmers Weekly* offered to supply dairy cows of the highest quality either for cash or on leasing or Hire-Purchase terms. The advert stated quite specifically that the cows would be delivered for approval on delivery! This was something quite new and reassuring for the buyer.

The very first customer rang up that Friday night to place an order. To my astonishment he wanted nearly *two hundred* cows, and altogether, over a period of two years - six hundred. I was in business with a vengeance. Without being asked he supplied the name and address of his bankers. My own bank could then make

'In the potato field'

the first of hundreds of subsequent inquiries and within a couple of days I learned that my man was "Quite undoubted" for the amount specified. This had been for a hundred thousand pounds. In the event my unknown first customer and I did business amounting to over a quarter of a million pounds before we met some years later. Conveniently he accepted my view that the best way to proceed would be to send two lorry loads a week until his requirements were met.

Within a few months I had developed a *modus-operandi* which remained unchanged for the next thirty years. I bought cows at Kendal on most Mondays, Penrith most Tuesdays, Annan on Thursdays and Carlisle on Fridays. Most nights I was answering phone-calls from all parts of the U.K. and establishing that essential rapport with prospective but unseen customers which would hopefully result in business,which might be quite substantial. This was in addition to my regular lorry loads to my unknown benefactor.

In addition I grew certified seed potatoes (although probably I was the one who should have been certified!) This business was being almost totally sewn-up by the big boys in much the same way as the developers and purveyors of genetically modified seeds are aiming to do now. I still bred my own livestock but to allow me to be away from home as and when required, I had had to sell the Guernseys and establish a herd of Herefords. They suckled their calves, and merely required the minimum of supervision especially in summer. Little did I suspect that within fifteen years they too would be becoming nearly obsolete. With the public's increasing awareness of fat, Herefords were giving way to the flavourless beef of lean-meat continental cattle.

What I offered was a service to farmers which would operate on ethical principles. I strongly emphasised that I wasn't a dealer. Cattle dealers have a reputation not altogether dissimilar to horse traders. So I never used the word 'dealer', for it was anathema. I charged a commission of 2% on the purchase price, and sent the actual auction invoice with the cattle, so that my customers knew what I was getting out of the transaction. And they knew what each individual animal had cost. The other reassuring feature was

Mr Kidd judging the Supreme Dairy Champion at the Westmorland County Show

that I offered delivery "for approval". Of course they naturally had to provide or pay for the transport. It was only after the cows had arrived in Caithness or Cornwall or wherever it was, and the customer had actually seen the cattle that he had to sign the cheque for the balance of his bill.

I unequivocally guaranteed satisfaction. Not an easy thing to do, with livestock, but if the very, very occasional cow wasn't up to standard in some way I offered full redress, even to the extent in a few extreme cases, of authorising the cow to be sent for slaughter as a casualty. I stood the ensuing loss, for there always was a loss. It could amount to the difference between a dairy cow and the value of a carcase; maybe several hundred pounds. But the next time I saw the farmer from whom I had originally bought the cow, and sooner or later I *would* see him, I would put it to him that he had a moral obligation, at the very least, of paying at least half the loss. Knowing that I would be buying cows whenever he was again selling, he would accept the logic of this and pay his share with as good grace as he could muster. Next time, he would make a point of warning me off a doubtful cow! So really it was "satisfaction guaranteed" for my customer. If a replacement was wanted, then I took it myself in my trailer, or would include it in a convenient load bound in that general direction.

Bank references varied; from say, maybe those of a member of the aristocracy, or perhaps a Member of Parliament, (whose references incidentally might be quite dodgy!) to a smallholder in South Wales who was "Good for your figure and purpose". Others might read "Respectable and trustworthy, but we cannot answer for your figure". While this was often a danger signal, it wasn't necessarily so. The man *might* have another account elsewhere with a large credit balance. So delicate negotiations would be needed to try and elucidate the truth. Often it might mean simply driving to the farm, wherever it was, and "calling on the way to somewhere" to weigh up the risks. The fact that a newish Jaguar or lots of expensive farm machinery were visible, didn't necessarily prove anything.

Even so, one such possibly doubtful customer whom I was asked to visit on behalf of an H.P. company had just sold his worst field to the National Coal Board for a six figure sum, to provide a site for an enormous slag heap, when I called ostensibly "by chance"- to investigate. He showed me the cheque and I ran him to the bank to pay it in! Then he postponed his order.

Another customer sent his completed order form and his modest deposit which enabled me to confirm that at least the balance would be covered. His proposal form to the Hire-Purchase company I mostly used, was accepted by them, and on this basis I bought the thirty Ayrshire cows and despatched them in two hired lorries. I was on my way to London that evening and told my customer that "in order to make it more private" I would call and witness his signature myself, and pick up the balance of the deposit which the finance company required him to pay me. And I would also witness the H.P.Agreement. Mostly however, the drivers did this.

I arrived at the Staffordshire farm, fortuitously just in time to see the cows unloaded and I was immediately struck by the very ad-hoc arrangements that had been made for their arrival, but nevertheless the farmer appeared to be very pleased with the cows and readily signed the H.P. Agreement for me to forward to the Company, and I departed with my cheque for £1,200, being the balance of the deposit.

There was something niggling me as I drove away, even though I knew that the H.P Company would have made their own extensive inquiries before accepting the proposed transaction, but on an impulse - as it was after banking hours - I put up for the night at the Derbyshire town where the man's bank was located - perhaps curiously, not his own nearby market-town - and cashed the cheque as soon as it opened next day, before proceeding on my journey with an unusually large amount of money on me.

My unworthy suspicions had obviously been unfounded, for I received my balance cheque from the H.P.Company in due course and then forgot about the incident. Over a year later however, a Police Inspector called for confirmation of the transaction and he told me that altogether my 'friend' had bought cattle to the tune of over £120,000 with dodgy cheques during the previous twelve months, from various sources including Auction Marts, which should have known better,and that the cows had simply disappeared from the face of the earth. None - except mine - had been paid for, and none were ever traced. No doubt my cheque for £1,200 would have been stopped if it hadn't been cashed the moment the bank opened. The Inspector added dryly that "by now he will be out of prison! He only got twelve months". He had never paid any of the monthly payments to the finance company, but they hadn't thought of mentioning it to me. I might just possibly have been able to retrieve something for them.

Another order came, for two loads; consisting of thirty cows. Mixed Ayrshire and Friesian cows this time. Good Ayrshires were getting more and more difficult to buy in any number. The Friesian breed was gaining ground and Ayrshires were gradually diminishing. An affluent-sounding client at a good address was accepted by the Finance Company without the slightest delay. I was enabled to go into Scotland and bought the cows which were despatched within a couple of days. The arrangement was that the balance of the deposit of £1000, would come back to me - together with the completed and signed H.P. Agreement - through the good offices of one of the two lorry drivers who would also have acted as witnesses to the Agreement. One driver would ring me from the Motorway and arrange a rendezvous to hand me the completed document as they drove back. That would enable me to be paid the balance in the course of the next few days.

The drivers and I had arranged to meet at 'around midnight' at the nearest junction on the M6. but my heart sank as the driver explained, "The boss's wife said that 'he' was away for a day or two. But he's going to post it!" he added reassuringly, as alarm bells started to ring for me.

In fact there *was* a letter from him two or three days later. The postman was early that Saturday morning, as I sat eating my breakfast. But the letter expressed great dissatisfaction with the cows and also claimed that the Hereford bull I had been asked to send was lame on his back legs, and therefore "couldn't do his job". He enclosed a list purporting to show the amount of milk given by each of the cows the previous day. None seemed to have given over three gallons a day. There was no mention of the deposit or the H.P.Agreement.

I finished breakfast and after one or two urgent jobs jumped into my car and headed south, arriving at the West-Country farm at about two o'clock. There was no response to my knocking at the door of the imposing manor-house, so I wandered round the farmyard and eventually found my bull looking over a loose-box door. I let him out into the yard and was able to confirm that his feet, at least, were in perfect order before putting him back into the box.

At this point the herdsman arrived to do the evening milking and, as is often customary on a Saturday afternoon, he had arrived "a bit early". I introduced myself, and said that I had heard from his boss that he was disappointed - to say the least - with the cow's milk yields. "None were giving even three gallons a day." The herdsman was non-committal but agreed that I could help him with the 'evenings' milking and that between us we would weigh and record the milk yields of the recent arrivals.

We had just finished milking and were 'swilling' the milking parlour down, when the owner arrived. I went up and introduced myself. His face was a study. "Now Mr Davis!" (not his real name) I said, briskly, "Your herdsman and I have just finished milking the cows and we have recorded the milk yields. You will be pleased to know that none have given less than twenty pounds of milk". He didn't look at all impressed so I repeated it. "That's about two gallons apiece,and that at half past two in the afternoon! As you know, this means that they will probably be giving at least *three* gallons each tommorow morning. Probably without exception. And after a day or two when they have settled down a bit more, some of them will probably be giving nearer six gallons a day!" I paused. He seemed quite flabbergasted and didn't reply.

"Now", I continued,"We'll just go into the house and you can sign the H.P. Agreement and give me that cheque for nine hundred pounds deposit, and I'll be off North again. Oh, by the way, I've had the bull out and walked him round the yard, and his feet seem perfect". We went into the house where he signed the Agreement, which I duly witnessed. He gave me my cheque and I drove away to start the three hundred and fifty mile journey home. He had never spoken once. Not even to offer me a cup of tea.

Chapter 19

St Michael's Well

It may be a bit confusing, for it's not a well at all. And it has absolutely nothing to do with the well-known chain store. It actually looks more like a small deep pond than a well. It must be at least thirty or forty feet across, and probably twelve or fourteen feet deep. From it a small beck flows to the river Eden, which it joins half a mile away. The"well" is constantly refilled from underground sources with water of the utmost clarity. It is almost hidden from view by a fringe of ancient alder trees. Every Ordnance- Survey map as far back as the mid nineteenth century gives it the distinction of being included.

The Eden takes one of its great curves here and no doubt it has often changed its course. As children we were told that in ancient times a church stood on this site, and that if a stone was thrown into the deep waters, a church bell would be heard ringing! This was on the unlikely assumption that one would achieve a direct hit on the bells with one's first throw. But we never heard the bell, and all the stones have now gone.

Curiously enough, less than half a mile away as the heron flies, stands the parish church of Addingham dating from the sixteenth century. Sadly, no church records older than those from 1675 have survived a fire. There is no village of Addingham. Just a church and a school. The church is called the Church of St Michael! Some water-worn and broken headstones stand in the porch, reputedly having been recovered from the river. Who knows, there may be something in the old tale. And it is highly likely that the river *will* have changed its course many, many times over the centuries. And the worn old crosses which were, according to legend "found in the bed of the river", include some which seem to be pre-Christian.

But we boys weren't interested in legends. We were all after the enormous trout which had lived in the Well for years. We could perch on the canopy of alder roots which extended outwards on the surface of the water, and watch for the big one.. The trout had undoubtedly come up the stream from the river when it was quite a little tiddler, and found the little sanctuary, where he could live in peace on other tiny trout and minnows which arrived regularly.

But now, eight or nine years later, he was a monster! And, of course, a cannibal. Opinions differed but the general view was that he would be at least four pounds in weight. Possibly five. We had tried him with every choice morsel in vain. It looked so easy, it was maddening to see one's best efforts rejected. It was possible to drop a maggot, on the finest possible tackle, right in front of his nose, but he would always drift disdainfully away, turning his nose up. But if a worm or maggot floating down free as 'ground bait', it would be devoured in seconds. Robert determined to get the old cannibal, by hook or by crook. And old Jack Jackson had given him an idea.

Jackson had served in what had been German East Africa in the first World War and had ill-advisedly related how the troops had thrown hand grenades into the Galana River to bring stunned fish to the surface, whenever they wanted to vary their diet. Robert argued to himelf that if he could remove the monster, he would be doing a favour to any poor little fishes which unwittingly entered the killing ground.

Robert's father had an old and extremely unsafe twelve bore shotgun which "hadn't to be used under any circumstances". The next time a scrap-iron man came, his father would get rid of it. It wasn't to be used by anybody.

He smuggled the gun from the house, together with a few twelve bore cartridges. In the old corrugated-iron shed at the top of the St Michael's field he loaded a cartridge, though with all its pellets removed. It wouldn't do at all to shoot the old devil! All the powder from the remaining cartridges was poured carefully down the barrel, followed by some newspaper, very well rammed home. Finally - to keep the water out - he inserted a large cork into the end of the barrel. After attaching a long string to the trigger in such a way that it could be pulled from a safe distance, the whole diabolical device was wrapped in an old rubber sheet.

It was time to take a careful stock of the risks involved. The best place for him to be when the string was pulled would be behind that fallen tree right by the water's edge. There might be a sort of miniature tidal wave. It was possible that he might get a bit wet, he thought, somewhat apprehensively. Perhaps it was too close after all. There was no point in taking stupid risks. Nobody knew where he was, he thought; they wouldn't know where to find the body!

The trunk of the fallen tree must be a easily a yard thick, he decided. Crouching down onto the moist earth, with his heart thumping he pulled the string. For a split second it seemed that there had been a misfire. Then there was the sound of a faint "phut" and an extremely large bubble quietly broke the surface. 'It was like someone breaking wind in the bath', he thought,' but not as loud'. Still trembling he pulled the package to the surface to see what had happened. The 'explosion' had only managed to blow the cork out!

Chapter 20

Mother and the Gin Case

The attic clearance took much more time and determination than I had thought, and now and again I paused to determine if it was really right to consign ones' history to the flames. So sometimes I was made unwillingly to pause. The photograph of my mother, for example, 'helping out' by driving a load of seed corn out to the field on the old David-Brown tractor, had been published in a war-time American newspaper under the title "Granny helps war effort" I had to keep it..

But looking a bit closer at the photo one can see or deduce quite a history of British agriculture. It was obviously early spring. Mother seems to be well wrapped-up to face the March wind. In the field she is heading for, someone is using a long drill. They *were* long, for the 'box' part - which held about two hundredweight bags of grain - was some fifteen feet long, and could 'swivel' to allow entry to the fields through the narrow gates then considered adequate, few of them being wider than eight feet. Gates would have been this width for two hundred and fifty years or more, but this was soon to change over about thirty years, first to ten feet, then twelve or even more as farm machines more than doubled in size.

The long grain 'box' had a series of holes through which the grain simply fell to the ground. The adjustable outlets - to be set hopefully, at the desired rate - were about eight inches apart. The adjustment wasn't as easy as it sounds, and few sowers of corn could claim that the optimum seed rate has always been achieved. One of my 'helpers' managed to completely empty the drill within about a hundred yards! As he came back for a refill and shame-facedly apologised for the waste involved I replied with a straight face "Oh, if you get a bucket you'll soon have it picked up".

ERM 55

Coming as close behind the drill as possible was a set of horse - drawn harrows whose object was to cover the seed corn with soil as soon as possible and thus also deter the wheeling crowds of rooks from their easy breakfast. Soon the drills were to have a change which would eliminate this waste, for they would be fitted with flexible tubes down which the corn dropped into a shallow drill and be immediately covered with soil thrown from a revolving saucer-shaped disk.

So let's say it's March. Cold but dry. Luckily for Mother the HelmWind, a curious but violent spring wind which can sometimes blow over the Eden Valley for weeks, has stayed away this year. Some say that because of its tell-tale precursor of a huge band of white cloud over the ridge of the Pennines, it resembles the Table Mountain phenomenon at Cape Town.

There's still a complete haystack in the stackyard and it now seems unlikely that it will be broken into this winter, for the Dutch-barn isn't yet empty. So in all probability, that hay won't be used until next winter. And the threshing machine won't have its canvas cover removed for use until next autumn. Within a decade, threshing machines will be superseded by the combine harvester, each with a series of tanker-like trailers travelling alongside to receive the corn shooting like water through huge auger-fed pipes. Total labour force, three. Nearly all of them enjoying the fruits of agricultural engineers, one of whose main aims has been to provide 'sitting down jobs'.

The David Brown tractor would easily drive the thrashing machine from a power-take-off pulley at the rear and had itself during the last few years replaced the somewhat much more exciting steam tractor from Lazonby.

To operate the thrashing machine in the picture meant gathering a team of.. let's see. One man on top to cut the bands of string round the sheaves and to 'feed' them into the voracious maw of the machine. If he does this correctly the fearsome 'hum' will be quite constant but if he drops most of a sheaf in 'one go' the change in the hum will be noted and commented on by wiseacres up to a mile away. Another man or maybe a land girl will fork the sheaves up to him. Sometimes this will even need two people, depending on the distance involved. Another pair of hands, or even two pairs, will be needed at the end on the right, where the straw comes out - either loose or preferably in 'bottles' - about the size of a man, and tied with twine at top and bottom. Yet another man at the other end of the huge machine will see that the sacks are full, before flipping over a hinged flap to direct the corn into the spare empty sack alongside, while securely tying the first bag with twine. This job is usually considered to be the perquisite of the 'boss'.

In the meantime one or two strong unfortunates will be wheeling the bags to the foot of the granary steps and then carrying the heavy bags up the stone stairs. The bags are more than their own weight! Two more are carrying the 'bottles' of oat straw - valuable winter fodder - some distance to whichever part of the Dutch-barn is vacant by this time of year. Say ten or twelve men then, all working hard. All of them, that is, except the boss who is taking off the corn bags as they fill, swiftly switching the 'chutes' over to direct the corn to the awaiting empty bag.

In the house the farmer's wife will be calmly preparing for the influx of a dozen or more hungry men for their dinners. The men who constitute the thrashing team will be neighbours who will expect and receive reciprocal help when they have their own thrashing day. My father remarked to one of the old travelling thresher team "I expect you will pretty often have Tatie-pot for dinner most days?" "Aye, Mr Kidd,we do!" he replied with conviction, "Its a fair treet 'git hyam on a Sunday 'n hev a kipper!"

A spin-off resulting from the gradual disappearance of the stack will be the sometimes quite alarming number of rats which will steadily be vacating the 'sinking ship' effect of the gradual but total removal of their warm and comfortable winter home.The excited dogs wait with ill-concealed impatience for the emergence of their quarry. Sometimes scores of rats and mice are killed with a quick shake and then dropped as yet another of the creatures makes a dash for safety.

What is that - almost elegant - curiously curved roof, on the right of the picture? That is the 'Gin-Case'. Absolutely nothing to do with alcohol. It is where the 'gin' was once situated. My Dictionary has it: 'Gin'; scheme, artifice, contrivance, a cotton gin'. The gin was the machine used to crush the corn so that it wouldn't wastefully pass straight through the ruminant's four stomachs undigested. So the oats were painstakingly fed into the gin, the crushing mechanism being powered by a horse which went round and round the semi circular 'gin-case'. The scene must have been almost biblical. But the building won't actually have been used for its original purpose since the days of Queen Victoria, for it wasn't designed for the entry of anything wider than a horse or a barrow. And that is why, like most of these old structures, the one in the photograph has now gone, and unless a few are preserved soon, for old time's sake, they won't even be a memory.

Chapter 21

Mucho Machísmo at Pamplona

We hadn't been able to find out who San Fermin was. There is a complete dearth of information about him, but naturally that is no reason why he shouldn't be celebrated in a big way. And that is a very considerable understatement, for the celebrations take up the whole of life in Pamplona for the second week of July. We had deemed it advisable therefore, early in March, in what we thought was good time, to look-up the local hotels in the Michelin Guide in order to book our night's stay.

We had a bit of a shock. "No Senor! We have absolutely no vacancies during San Fermin week for at least another ten years!" And one by one the other hotels confirmed this position. It *might* - just possibly - have been different if we had intended staying for a full week, but we could only spare one day as we had to catch the auto-rail at Biarritz the following day. Many hotels have block bookings for whole families for every San Fermin week in perpetuity.

Eventually we had managed to book-in at the Parador at Olite, thirty miles away. We arrived outside the main door of the historic old castle, after driving from Teruel. It had been very much overlong as is often the case in Spain where distances seem to have no relation to those on the map. We arrived at long last in one of the heaviest rainstorms of my life. The drops of rain were the size of damsons, and they were very close together. We were forced to sit in the car and wait for half an hour before we could dash to the hotel doorway only, a yard away, for cover.

In view of the thirty odd miles involved I asked for an early call - something apparently quite unheard of in Paradors - but was assured by the dour receptionist that he himself, personally, would ensure that I was in time for the day's events in Pamplona which start with the running of the bulls to the Plaza de Toros.

The Parador staff in general seemed to be on the dour side. When I noticed that there were only two wrapped portions of butter set out on our table for the three of us, and asked for more 'mantequila, por favor?' the little waitress replied icily "Dos para tres!" Two for three! Later I regretted not asking her to actually divide it for us.

When I awoke it was already past six o'clock; the time I had requested for my call and I found the receptionist fast asleep on a couch behind the desk. It looked as if he intended to make a day of it so there seemed to be little point in rousing him from his deep sleep, or even in suggesting that he should in all fairness return the *propina* of two hundred pesetas which I had given him in advance the night before. I dashed for the car and headed up the Autopista to Pamplona hoping to avoid the rush.

Not a chance! The whole place was buzzing with activity and I realized that my wild idea of trying to negotiate a place on a friendly balcony was absolutely absurd. Anyway, all the balconies seemed dangerously overcrowded as it was! The whole town was absolutely heaving with excited humanity. And it wasn't yet seven o'clock in the morning.

There was no option but to be carried along by the solid mass of humanity which was heading for the Plaza de Toros. I was swept into the bull-ring swiftly past the rough-hewn statue of Ernest Hemingway, the great *aficionado* himself, and into the famous bull ring which he did so much to publicise. Amazingly the place was almost full! Eighteen thousand people were already assembled. The torrential rain of the night before had left all the concrete seats dripping. All the cushions in the place had already been hired. So an enterprising newspaper seller was clearing his stocks of the "Diario de Navarra" like hot cakes. All I wanted one for, was to provide something dry to sit on. But somehow I still have my copy. Men were working desperately down in the arena - the word itself was a bit confusing for us, for it is also the Spanish word for 'Sand'. There were waggon-loads of dry sand with which they were trying to sop-up the wettest areas. In another corner a troupe of tumblers was desperately trying, but failing, to entertain the crowd and a band was belting out the paso-dobles for dear life. There was an unconcealed air of excitement pervading the place.

Then the band stopped playing. The entertainers disappeared and there was a profound silence as everyone strained to hear the explosion of the rocket which would be the signal that the bulls were coming. They come through the designated traditional route through the crowded streets. There is no traffic except for police cars and ambulances. But with the six bulls of the Toros Bravos breed running for their appointment with death that night, come at least as many, emasculated, bulls. Bullocks; which have done this run before - and which will do it again next day! These treacherous animals are *cabestros* - a Spanish word which also has come to mean 'leading by the nose'. Some of them even have bells and are routinely used to help in the handling of the powerful 'toros bravos',which will unknowingly be galloping towards their deaths before nightfall. In its report of the Millenium events the Guardian has a wonderful photo of the bulls running. But one of these animals in the photo must be a bullock, for it is clearly wearing a bell! But to the runners and - it seems - to a large number of press photographers, they are all bulls. In any case there is no time for a clinical examination. Keep on running!

And in front of the dozen or more bulls, and the bullocks, of course - already thundering along the barricaded streets are dozens, scores, even hundreds of young men in white with the red neckerchiefs and sashes traditional to the event and armed only with rolled-up newspapers which, in theory at least, will enable anyone to defend oneself against half a ton of beef hurtling itself along a narrow calle. All this and the wide, sharp, curling horns a yard or two from one's posterior is supposed to give anyone a remarkable turn of speed.

The side roads have been blocked with temporary fences of heavy planks, thick as railway sleepers. The uprights of these 'fences' are set in purpose-made steel sockets, which are permanent fixtures in the road. These barriers, all the balconies, and every available vantage point has its load of excited spectators.

Soon the first of the *aficionados* enters the arena. This small handful appear to be slightly embarrassed by the distance which they have quite wisely put between themselves and the bulls, and they enter the ring somewhat sheepishly, to jeers and cat-calls, for there is to be quite a perceptible pause before those who are really running in earnest arrive and trot into the *Plaza de Toros*. Those firstcomers must have set off running long before the gun went off. They will never live it down!

Now come red-faced runners, a shade faster, puffing and blowing. But one or two seem unaturally pale. Some have fallen on the way. Some have been trodden on or even gored, and some will have been taken away in waiting ambulances. For news of that we will have to await the evenings' early edition of the *Diario de Navarra*. The rest of the youths, who have survived unscathed - so far - part to each side of the arena as the bulls and their treacherous companions - which will live to run again many times - pass into the corrals at the back of the arena. There the bulls will rest and spend a quiet day, incidentally emptying their stomachs in readiness for their final public appearance that night, because as soon as the teams of brightly decorated mules have dragged the carcases of the recently despatched toros from the ring, these will go to the adjacent abattoir where the butchers wait to dress the carcasses which will then pass on to local butchers. There seems no evidence here of the horrendously expensive qualified vets who have, by law, to 'supervise' every stage of operations in British slaughter-houses.

The patrons of the best hotels will have wined and dined well, overwell, like nearly everyone else in the town, until the early hours but in the "Yoldi", one of their favourite hotels, the matadors will also pass a hungry day. Their stomachs too, will have to be empty - just in case something goes wrong and surgery is required. It is not surprising that the name of Alexander Fleming is held in the highest esteem in Spain and especially in bull-fighting circles. There must be hundreds and possibly thousands of Spanish streets now named after the discoverer of penicillin. And on the premises is an emergency operating theatre.

But back in the arena itself the youths mill-about excitedly, chatting over the more spectacular events of the run. I begin to wonder if that is all there is to it. Suddenly it all seems rather flat and it isn't yet eight o-clock! Without any warning a door opens and a very small wiry heifer, maybe about a year old, of the Toros Bravos breed shoots out into the arena like a projectile! On its small but quite dangerous horns it is wearing a pair of stiff-leather 'covers' something like glorified 'finger-stalls', presumably as some sort of protection, but giving it a most ungainly appearance as it races round the ring.

Several youths go down or are tossed into the air in seconds as they strive to avoid the speeding animal. The 'finger-stalls' seem remarkably ineffective. One lad - maybe in an alcoholic belief in his abilities as a torero - stamps a foot as he shakes his small red handkerchief in challenge. 'Ha! Toro!'. But a speeding heifer misses him only by inches and there is a roar of applause from the crowd, but the heifer quickly turns round in less than its own length and sends him flying. After a few more hectic minutes two daring youths get their arms round the neck of the pugnacious animal and it is manhandled, with due respect, from the ring.

By this time, however, there are serried rows of youths squatting side by side, right in front of the door from which another heifer will shortly be hurling itself. It seems absolutely suicidal. It is almost as if all these youths are determined to end the morning with at least one "honourable" scar, which will ensure that their names will be listed as "*asistidos en la infirmaria*" that night. The paper I had been sitting on details about twenty such incidents from the previous morning's event. These reports will be regarded as badges of honour and machismo.

But there *are* many other things at Pamplona, except bulls, and wine in prodigious quantities. Every day - for a whole week - there are innumerable activities, many of them on a much more cultural plane. There are concerts, musical festivals, band contests, art exhibitions, children's choirs and orchestras. The list is almost endless. In fact the events have to start at six-thirty in the morning and they will continue until midnight. Then it is time for the dances to start. A full week at Pamplona must take a lot of stamina!

But I had to retrace my way back to the Parador to collect my compliment of passengers and luggage and head north again for Biarritz and the auto-rail home.

Chapter 22

Night at the Inn With the Croglin Vampire

He was a "commercial traveller" although that is a term rarely heard nowadays. More often than not they prefer to be called the "Northern Area Representative" or maybe "Sales Executive", but this man who had sought our aid didn't try to sell us a thing! He looked completely shattered, as if he'd had a very bad night. As indeed he had. A little earlier we had towed his car from a flooded road with our old Ferguson tractor and dried it out with a hot-air blower. Now it was almost ready to go and finally spluttered and started albeit rather hesitantly. I put his battery on our fast charger while he had his 'ten o'clocks' with us. As he seemed more relaxed he told his tale.

"I had to confess to myself that I was absolutely lost", said the Sales Representative. "I expect you heard the gale blowing last night. It was a real howling gale. The rain was absolutely coming down in buckets. Deceptively deep pools of rain threatened to swamp my car altogether. Finally it gave up the unequal struggle. The electrics had completely packed up. I knew the battery was a bit dodgy, to say the least, so I didn't keep pressing the starter. Someone once told me that in a case like that the best thing to do was to sit still for a few minutes and the residual heat of the engine would be enough to dry out the soaked plug-leads or whatever it was that had caused the stoppage".

"But not a bit of it! The starter was dead and the lights wouldn't work. I was miles from anywhere. But maybe not, I thought. There was what appeared to be a light flashing about two hundred yards away. On second thoughts it wasn't flashing at all. The flashing effect must have been caused by the branch of a tree waving violently in the gale. Then there was another bright flash of lightning which was followed almost immediately by prolonged and frightening peals of thunder. That one must have been really close, because the flash and the bang were practically simultaneous."

"But the brilliant lightning had given me a split-seconds' view of the source of the 'flashing' light. There actually *was* a house there with a light above the door. A handful of people were running to their cars. Obviously a country pub! Great! There was no point in even thinking about it. I grabbed my briefcase, locked up the car and ran for it. I was almost there - over a small hump-backed bridge - when the light over the door went out. I hammered like mad at the door. Eventually I could just hear sounds of someone coming, and I could hear the bolts being drawn. 'What hev ye ferggiten?' It was a man's voice grumbling, evidently thinking that I was one of his late customers. I quickly put in my plea for help. 'Come on in then!' he said, reluctantly, as he led the way along the dark hall into the bar which was lit only by the dying embers of what had been a real roaring log fire. 'Dus't want summat to drink?' he asked, brusquely."

"I had to move pretty cautiously through the obstacles of tables stools and chairs, to the bar to watch him draw my pint. I noticed that he left the end of his thumb over the top of the glass and I realized that he was quite blind! The end of his thumb was telling him when the glass was full. I expect you probably know him anyway. I once heard of a blind landlord. Might even be the same one!"

"The landlord asked 'bacon and eggs alright?' It was a statement, just a formality, for without waiting for a reply he went off to the kitchen. I moved over to the fire which had now been restored and was crackling away nicely. 'Put thi wet coat ower that chair and sit down and warm thisel up a bit. What thou wants is a large rum afore thou hes out else'. The speaker was an old man sitting by the fire, and he was obviously well practised in the art of giving a hint. He offered to bring it from the bar and didn't hesitate in accepting my offer of one for himself. He seemed a companiable soul."

'At this point the landlord returned with the bacon and eggs. "Mind" he said, 'the plate's really hot. I'll sit aside ye and keep you company". He seemed to have toned down his Cumbrian dialect quite a bit for my benefit, for which I was grateful. He turned to the old man; 'It's time you were going up, Dad, it's nearly midnight.' And without any argument, the old chap went off to bed. He seemed to have had quite a good night." "My rescuer stayed sitting by the fire, after I had finished eating, while the house seemed to shake with the wind. The rain was hurtling against the window almost like bullets. He stirred the fire again and threw another log on. I was already feeling much better. Then he told me what he said was an authentic local ghost story. Maybe it was just to settle me for the night".

"The landlord seemed to hesitate before he launched into the tale. 'The farm where it all happened,' he said eventually, 'is just about half a mile away, down the beck. It's just over living memory ago, cause mi father knew awe aboot it. There used to be two brothers farming the place, and their young sister had become, really, the mistress of the place since her mother had died a year or two before'. 'Yan wild night, they used to say, maybe yan just like this - except that it had been snowing earlier on - the lass was wakened-up by a queer sort of scratching sound at her bedroom window. She got hersel out of bed and went to t'window, peering out into t' night wid a flickering candle, as if that would help her!"

"There, outside the window and pretty obviously perched on a ladder, was a man. He had to be standing on summat! That was bad enough but it wasn't just that. He had the most frightful face she had ever seen. His mouth opened in a snarl. His teeth, what there was of them, would have been a dentist's nightmare. T'lass screamed and just aboot collapsed in a heap on't floor. Later on when she got her voice back, she said "the teeth were like a crocodiles"! Her two brothers rushed intil her bedroom to see whativer was t'matter. She couldn't even speak except for gasps but pointed, sort of hysterically at t'window which t'younger brother managed to open just in time to see a curious stooping figure of a man scurrying across t'yard. They chased him of course, but it was a useless chase. Finally Nathan - t'elder brother of t'lass, said that they had better go back."She's all on her own", he said, "He might have doubled back to t'house". But the lass hadn't been harmed, although she was terrible upset. She had put on her dressing gown and had had the sense to get the old double-barrel twelve bore shotgun which she was nursing on her knees".

"After a week or two t'brothers were coming to t'conclusion that maybe it had awe been imagination. But she wouldn't have that at all and so they had to continue wid their "sentry" duties, taking turn and turn aboot".

"Then there was another bit of snow, and funnily enough t'Helm wind started to blow. It's not often you git both on them together', he chuckled, 'My old Dad used to say it could blow the neb off a goose!' Then he carried on with the tale. 'That night', he said, after giving the fire a poke, 'there was another horrible scream from t'lass's bedroom. The brother who was supposed to be "on watch", managed to shake himself awake and leaned out of his own window. What he saw there, perched on the highest rungs of the farm ladder and leaning against the girl's bedroom window was what seemed to be a figure like a gorilla!".

'The landlord had to stop at that point to fill up our glasses and stir the last embers of the fire. "Aye!" he continued, "the girl's brother poked the gun out of the window and took a quick shot and the "gorilla", "villain", call it what you like, fell to the ground moaning, but picked hissel up and with a funny sort of shuffling trot managed to cross t'yard and disappeared into the night". The two brothers slipped on their coats and boots, and the two of them set off to catch or even kill whatever it was that they were following. It was easy at first to follow the trail in the snow but the cunning beggar had been clever enough to make use of those bits of the lane which had mainly blown clear of snow. Their stable lamp was just about useless but the moonlight helped quite a bit."

"At the finish they ended-up in Croglin churchyard. They could easily follow the tracks, for by now the snow had got deeper. Now the footprints could be seen quite clearly as they led to the old part of the burial ground - it won't have been used for a hundred years or more - and they ended-up at a moss covered stone tomb.'

He stopped speaking at that point, and I stayed quiet. I didn't want to spoil his train of thought".

'The landlord emptied his glass. Mine was already empty and my throat was unbelievably dry. "It took both of them" he said eventually, "to lift the heavy stone flag from the tomb". 'What was there?" I asked eagerly. I couldn't help it. "Well", he said, a bit reluctantly, as if he didn't want to come to the end of the story, "They shone the miserable little light of their lamp down into the tomb. There was a shrivelled sort of parchment-like, mummified corpse with a face that they would never forget for the rest of their lives. Through the centre of the chest, maybe driven through, years and years ago, was an old wooden stake. And that's about it" he said, ending his tale thoughtfully and added, as an afterthought."Oh, yes. There *was* a trickle of fresh blood running slowly from the side of his mouth!".

"I think it's time for bed, for both of us", he said cheerfully as he led the way confidently up the dark stairs. He had completely forgotten to switch on any lights. But it was all the same to him, I thought. He opened a bedroom door for me,"That's yours, Goodnight!" he said. Entering the bedroom I reached for the switch. Nothing happened. 'There must have been a power cut after all', I thought! I felt my way into bed, fully clothed and shivered as I felt the damp sheets. I was desperately tired but I couldn't sleep. There was something - I couldn't quite be certain what it was - but there was something scratching - maybe possibly just a branch - scratching at the window.'

Chapter 23

Camels and Mules

Everybody laughed when I fell off the camel as it kneeled down - grunting as if in pain - in response to some gutteral Arabic command. To be precise I didn't actually fall off, I slid gently down its long neck and the ugly great animal leered at me with its horrible stained teeth. With as much dignity as I could command, which actually wasn't much when I was wearing a red fez -which the grinning Moroccan camel man had popped on my head - I could only try and grin foolishly as if I would do it again anytime.

We had had a day-trip from Algeciras, the Spanish port next to Gibraltar. The whole place has an profound air of illegality about it. One can almost smell it in the air. And one feels certain that every parked lorry contains - or is waiting for - a load of illegal immigrants. For nearly every morning, bodies of those who didn't quite make it are found washed-up onto the beach. Bodies of what are now termed 'economic migrants'. People who have trekked from all over Africa full of hope. Now they are washed up like flotsam. Others, more fortunate, are working where few others will, in the intense heat of the plastic covered desert of Almeria so that some supermarket can provide us with an all year round supply of spring vegetables.

But there must have been a fiesta somewhere because little girls brightly dressed in traditional style were being escorted home by their proud mothers. The receptionist at the Octavio hotel had assured us that we would all be able to board the fast hydrofoil which was scheduled to leave for Tangier in twenty minutes. They had said categorically that as long as we had valid passports there would be room for us.

We could actually pay the *recepcionista*. They had an 'arrangement'. There is something very obliging about Spanish hotels.

She had arranged for a taxi to pick us up and we arrived at the quayside just in time to take our seats. They were actually the last available. So far so good. We cast off and in a few minutes we were skimming over the calm sea to the west of the great mass of the Rock of Gibralter, which rears up somehat surprisingly to nearly 1,400 feet above sea level. The sea was like glass and we were heading south west comfortably at nearly forty miles an hour. Soon we were joined by a small school of dolphins which easily kept up with us, it seemed, just for the fun of it.

The Rock is a hugely emotive issue for nearly all Spaniards who seem to fully support intermittent measures - not much more than aggravations - in support of having it returned to Spain while arguing that there is no basis whatsoever for returning the Spanish North African enclaves of Melilla and Ceuta to Morocco! But soon Gibralter was far behind and we were approaching the African coast.

The guide, a Moroccan in a long black shirt, spoke several West European languages and took complete charge of us, starting off by collecting everyone's passport which he said he would have in his safe keeping until we got back on the hydrofoil. Uneasily we all handed these valuable items over to him for the day. We toured the Casbah like a small Sunday School outing, under the charge of an anxious teacher, and watched a snake charmer doing his stuff with a cobra. Every now and then the guide would do a head-count. Then we went for lunch, and the roast lamb and cus-cus were delicious. Coffee came in absurdly small cups as the belly dancer tried to impress us. She had been a raving beauty, no doubt, twenty years earlier and three stones lighter. But even so she was still remarkably agile. Someone averred that she would be able to crack a nut with her belly-button.

We passed into a covered market, full of tourist tack of all descriptions and copper vessels of every shape and size. I took a fancy to a copper 'water-pot' and naturally, in spite of feigned lack of interest, almost to the point of boredom, was spotted almost immediately by the dusky proprietor."You; English - French-American?" he asked urgently. "English. Right! What you want, copper pot eh?" I made out that it was merely of passing interest, only a fad, but these chaps are no fools.

"I don't actually want it, but how much would a pot like this cost?" I asked trying to be vague about it. "Ninety English pounds, cheap, very very cheap!" "Move on a bit," I murmured to Pamela, "try not to look keen!" We did several circuits of the market and at every circuit he lowered the price. I began to remember how my father used to buy cattle on farms, even going to the length of getting into the car and slamming the door. Sometimes he even bade me to drive away before relenting and increasing his final bid by a fraction.

It was actually quite a large handsome copper pot, and our car; waiting at Algeciras, would have room for it. Nearly everyone else had a return air-trip at the back of their minds. Eventually the deal was closed at twenty seven English pounds, and fifty pence. Oh Yes. He would accept any currency. We carried our prize away, carefully wrapped in Arabic newspaper trying to still look doubtful. To reach the Hydrofoil we had to run the gauntlet of about twenty optimistic street vendors who hoped we would still have some money left. Eventually we had an uneventful trip back and having our passports safely returned seemed like a bonus.

Next day we drove from Algeciras up the mountain road towards Ronda and I stopped the car near Benalauria to ask an old lady if I could sketch her little cottage, for a subsequent painting. 'Not much of a picture', she said. But I sat on the grass by the roadside and sketched. Soon an old man appeared leading a cow by a halter. I could see at a glance that the cow was in season and in fact he confirmed that he was just returning the cow from a visit to the communal parish bull, and hoped that this time she would be pregnante. He couldn't understand how I - 'who said he was a farmer'- could be on holiday in Spain. He never had had a holiday nor had he ever wanted one.

Down the valley from Benalauria where we were conversing, as best we could, there was an enormous eucalyptus forest. These fast growing trees have proliferated in Spain in recent decades and this valley of mature trees was now being felled. As we talked what might well be the last mule-train in Spain came up from the bottom. Each splendid mule would be probably carrying two or three hundredweight with apparent ease. They marched over, unasked, to the large heap of logs and waited patiently to have the slip-knots undone. The mules worked well with the minimum of supervision. Twenty years later one can drive right across Spain without seeing a single mule or donkey. That's progress.

Senora Garcia waved us all into the house. The interior would not have differed much from one or two or three hundred years ago. With the grace of a duchess she poured all of us a glass of wine. Pamela and her mother - having no Spanish - had to smile quite a lot and kept saying *gracias*. Later on when I had 'finished' my picture in oils at home - as far as I was able to, that is - I sent them a photo of the framed picture, and received a letter of warm thanks, in English, from one of their daughters who worked in a Gibraltar hospital.

We had booked-in at the Hotel Reina Victoria, in Avenida Dr Fleming. (Yet another of the tributes to the discoverer of penicillin!) But it wasn't our own Queen Victoria - although the place certainly had an English Victorian ambience - perched on the very edge of the vast cliff at Ronda, and from our room we could look down through the safety rails six hundred feet to the farmers toiling in their little plots below. It was like a microcosm of Spanish agriculture. It wouldn't have changed all that much since the days of George Borrow. The last time we were in Ronda there was talk of making not one, but *four*, golf courses! To my new friend Garcia it would be sacrilege to even consider such a thing, to say nothing about the waste of precious irrigation water which would be needed.

Further north, much further, we spent quite some time looking for the site of the actual battle which is commemorated as Arroyo Day by the Border Regiment. The 'Battle' of Dos Molinos near Placencia during the Peninsular campaign may in fact have been only a skirmish, but it won't be forgotten in Carlisle. Our trouble was that every watercourse is an Arroyo - usually dry in summer - and the actual location of the 'Two Mills' is now difficult to determine.

When we got back in the car it was sweltering, so all windows were immediately opened wide. Passing Bejar en route for the Sierra de la Peña de Francia, the 'mountains of the sorrows of France' all the windows were shut as we passed through a cloud of dust raised by some roadworks. All, that is, except one which stubbornly refused to close. Electric windows may be very convenient but this was highly inconvenient and potentially serious for there would be little point in locking-up.

Nearing the Sierra de Gata -'Cat Mountain' - we chanced on a garage which seemed to be specialising in Land-Rovers, so we pulled in on the off-chance that they might do something for our Rover."What a coincidence", they said, "that B.M.W. which drove away as you arrived had just had exactly the same trouble!" Although by now it was their 'dinner-hour' two men dismantled the interior of the door thus revealing the 'works'. "Aha!" they said, after diagnosing the fault," We can't mend it. "Our collective hearts sank.

"But", said the man who was seeing his dinner-hour disappearing by the minute, "what we *will* do is to change the little motors round so that the faulty motor which normally shuts the window, is swapped for the one which normally opens it!" This was done in what was the rest of the man's dinner-hour and the button was pressed. To our great relief the window closed. That it wouldn't open again until we got home was a minor inconvenience. At least we could lock our car. Our saviour had to be pressed hard to accept a small token of our appreciation.

We motored on - greatly relieved - over the Sierra de Gata - to find that half the young forest had been burnt in what must have been a violent conflagration. Several square miles were just ashes in spite of the miles and miles of 'fire-breaks' which some expert had decreed would be sufficient.

At length we pulled-in, to our enormous surprise, to what was evidently a picnic area. The first we had ever seen in Spain. After we had availed ourselves of its facilities and were about to tidy up and leave, Pam said in a note of urgency. "There's a man there behind that tree, with a gun pointing at us!" And there *was* a man there! But he was merely having a piddle onto the tree! And the 'rifle' was only his walkie-talkie.

He walked over and was most friendly. "Aha! You're an artist" he said - observantly - as he saw me packing a few canvases carefully into the boot. "You should come and paint my house. It's so picturesque." Somewhat intrigued I asked him for the name of his village and looked it up on the map. In the event we turned off the road to Cuidad Rodrigo - our evening's destination - and I asked for the house of Senor Gerado. It was, however a bit of a disappointment for the house was lacking the Spanishness I wanted. But by then it seemed that the whole population of the village was at my back to see for themselves the creation of a 'masterpiece'! They were intrigued at the choice of subject. As I hesitated the proud owner swept into the street on his little red motor-bike, for he hadn't been able to match our speed. There was no option but to continue with the painting. I emphasised that it would have to be completed back home in England. Here I could only sketch. Within half an hour we were on our way to the waves of our new friends.

In the event the picture was a disappointment. There was nothing of note in it. So I painted an ox cart standing in the shade of the wall and the picture seemed transformed. I liked it anyway. So I took a snap of the painting and posted it, with my compliments, to the Gerados. In due course there was a reply thanking me. The letter was polite and very formal. I felt sure that he would much rather that I had put his shiny red motor bike leaning against the wall.

There was a sequel to our brief trip to Africa. We had researched the Penninsula Campaign at Cuidad Rodrigo, and then at some length casually examined the ravines on the edge of the Puerta Piedrafita down which the treasure chests of the army retreating to La Corruna had allegedly been thrown by the defeated British columns and sadly, failed to find any trace. Now it was time to get back to Santander to catch the ferry home. At Plymouth we opted for the 'Nothing to Declare' exit but were pulled in to face the customs. They opened our cases and searched zealously through all our soiled linen, opened out all the socks, inserted probing fingers into our spare shoes. They unwrapped the Arabic newspaper from the copper pot and turned it upside-down. It was a very, very thorough examination. Others appeared to be ready to take the car into its component parts.

All the while my dear little mother-in-law - a model of an English grandma - lectured them. She was really cross. I'd never seen her like that. 'They should be ashamed of themselves', she said, 'wearing those uniforms!' (And they did closely resemble naval uniforms!) Her husband 'had been in the Battle of Jutland!' she said. The relevance of the remark escaped them!

At length one of the team turned gently towards her and said, "We are only doing our job, Madam. After all, your passports show you've been to Morocco! These cases could have been absolutely full of contraband; drugs, heroin or cannabis, you name it. You could have been getting away with murder! And that copper pot alone could have held millions of pounds worth! But I think you are a charming Engish lady, and we do apologise for all this trouble!".

Chapter 24

Old Albert and the Black Pudding

There was no doubt that Albert was a hard-headed business man. A *small* business man, it is true; but he had many of the attributes of men who are household names. But it was mainly as a bicycle repair man that he was known to us youngsters, at a time when a new bike was something beyond most boys' wildest dreams. And those of us who were lucky enough to actually posess a hand-me-down bike, considered we were in the fortunate few, even if we could only reach the pedals by putting one's foot through under the top-bar to reach the offside pedal.

Albert hardly ever actually bought any spare parts but would return from his closely guarded sources with the gears, spokes, cones with which he woud do our repairs. In addition he did quite a number of odd jobs including delivering morning papers to several households including ours. So it was fairly obvious that Albert had to 'go on the list' when we had our bi-annual pig killing. He would have to be included in Mother's largesse.

Like most folk who killed their own pigs we had the usual problem of somehow disposing of the enormous amount of 'pig-stuff' before it 'went-off'. There was no problem with the sides of fatty bacon - and they were *fatty*! Sometimes there would only be one thin - very thin - streak of lean in a whole rasher! Nobody would eat it now. But the sides and hams would safely hang on the ceiling hooks for up to maybe twelve months. And the 'pig cheek'- the bit that corresponds to a human 'double-chin was father's favourite. It was sacrosanct. But it was the rest that could give real problems, for it would still be several years before elctricity would come to the village. And a deep-freeze was beyond imagination - let alone a fridge!

The usual way to get rid of any surplus; to immediate require ments, that is, was to give it to relatives and friends, who firstly, killed a pig of their own ,and secondly and most importantly, would be likely to reciprocate when they themselves had a pig-killing. Sometimes this proved to be a folorn hope.

Years later, for some obscure reason, I described the whole process of the pig-killing to a stranger sitting opposite me in 'Ill Fornello', a favourite little Italian restaurant in Southampton Row. This was when I was in London most months for Potato Marketing Board meetings; being an elected member for the Northern Counties. 'Il Fornello' was my usual restaurant because, curiously, most of the waiters were Spanish! And as I was learning Spanish at the time, I eventually got to know them quite well, including the head-waiter, Jesus Gomez. When Pamela and I stayed a night at the old pilgrim's stop-over - the sixteenth century Hostal San Marcos, now a Parador - in his home town of Leon, we even paid a visit to his parents. They recieved us with delight and traditional Spanish hospitality.

'Il Fornello' was filling-up rapidly and Jesus asked to be excused for packing-in a young couple at the end of our small table. I returned to my story and had just reached the bit where I was describing how as a seven-year old boy, it was my task to stir the blood - every drop of which would be required to make the black-puddings - as it poured from the pig, thus preventing it from coagulating, when there was a sudden choking sound from one of the newcomers as he managed to blurt-out 'Do you mind? We're vegetarians!'

After our pig-killing Mother had prepared a little parcel of real Cumberland sausages and some black-pudding ready for Albert when he delivered our morning papers. More than a week passed by, with Mother waiting in vain, for some hopefully appreciative comment, until finally in desperation she asked him outright. 'How did you like the sausage and black-pudding, Albert?' Albert had evidently given the matter some thought. 'Oh!'he said ' ' ' 't'sausages were a la-al bit ower peppery, n't black-puddin hed aw't fat at ya end!'

Just how peppery sausage should be, has always been a contentious issue. But in the fifties when I sold some fat sows (from which most sausage is made) I was incensed enough to write to my local paper, the '*Cumberland and Westmorland Herald*' forcibly pointing out the enormous disparity between the prices received by the primary producer; me, for fat sows, and the prices charged for sausage by the butcher.

At the market the following week I was angrily accosted by Stanly, our local butcher. 'Hey! That letter of thine in't Herald about t'price of sausages! Well, there's ya thing thou's completely fergotton aboot!' 'Oh! What that, then, Stanley?" I asked. Back came the shattering riposte; *the coup de grâce;* 'Pepper's got awful dear, lately!'

As a strong young man Albert had moved with his family to a Lancashire town where one of my aunts lived. Aunt Ada thought it would be a nice gesture, and like a breath of home to have them for high tea. Albert had been briefed that he would be expected to make at least some contribution to the conversation instead of silently ploughing through his meal. Unless he had been well-primed there would have been no chance whatever of what might turn out to be sparkling conversation. He would eat silently and well, lost, perhaps, in thought.

Eventually conscious of warning glances from his mother, Albert cleared his throat. It was now or never. 'By goy!' he said, 'It's a bit of tebble poor cheese you've got hold of!'

Back in Lazonby there was a new Co-op manager, George Sisson, who sorted out the mess left by an absconding predecessor and put the place on a sound business footing. His son Ronnie and I formed a sort of partnership to buy our own motor transport. Albert had an old motor bike for sale; an old, very old motor bike for sale.It was a ancient belt driven 'Ivy', *circa* 1916 or thereabouts and it cost us thirty shillings. That we could even contemplate a purchase of such magnitude must have meant that Ronnie and I had just completed a week of back-breaking potato picking, during the annual holliday for that specific pupose. I can't remember. But I do remember that I put a pound towards its purchase while Ronnie became the 'junior partner' with a contribution of ten shillings.

There was a little petrol in the tank, so we wheeled it cautiously across the road into our long meadow, and without much trouble started it up. Then we spent an hour or more circling the meadow taking it in turns, and even riding sometimes with one, on what passed for the pillion. We rode, at speeds of up to twenty miles an hour over the narrow stone flag, which formed a bridge over the beck. It seemed like crossing the Niagara Falls on a tightrope!

Then we ran out of petrol. There was no chance whatsoever of raising the one shilling and six pence for a gallon of petrol so we wheeled the machine home.

Home, of course meant the home of the majority shareholder.This went without saying. So we wheeled it up our drive. Father had just been feeding the pigs and as was customary, was wearing the 'coarse-apron' he used for that purpose. 'What have you got there?' he said. We thought it was obvious, but replied politely. 'A motor bike!' 'Where did you get it?' 'Old Albert's' 'Take it back!' said Father. Father never repeated himself. We knew that it was the end of the conversation!

Back at Albert's however we found that there had been a sudden crash in the value of second-hand motor bikes. All we could recover was a pound! (..and No! I have no idea where it is now!)

Chapter 25

An Ounce of Blue Vitriol

The old man in the bar looked at his empty glass, as if somewhat puzzled that it hadn't been refilled, but he went on with his story. "Ah know you might not believe it, but it was a gai big family. Twenty three bairns! All under thirty, but there was summat else! They all stuttered! Trouble was that as the bairns grew old enough to talk, they copied their older brothers or sisters, till it ended up wid every yan on them stuttering! They were a grand lot of bairns; happy and contented with their lot. And they were a lot!" He paused but nobody laughed, so he went on with the tale. "Somebody cawed it an 'unfortunate affliction' but really it was mair of a sort a stoppage. They couldn't git started but yance they gat ga-en, it aw came out wid a rush!"

One of the visiting fishermen edged along the bar towards the speaker."You say that all twenty three children had this impediment, and that they 'caught it' from their elder brothers or sisters. But who did the eldest one catch it from?" He muttered a quiet aside to his companion, "Now I've got the old beggar!" The old man gave another glance at his empty glass and the fisherman nodded to the barman, who silently drew another pint. "Well, thank you! Who did t'eldest yan catch it frae? Well, t'was only natural. *He* caught it frae his mother! She couldn't say 'No!' fast enough!!" When the burst of laughter had died down, he added "Aye, when she couldn't say “No!" fast enough, she just said "N'niver mind!"

Times were getting very hard for farmers like Joe, the father of the enormous brood. Nowadays a family of that size would qualify for more 'benefits' in a week than he had ever made in a couple of months. He had to go bankrupt, and there was no alternative to leaving the farm. If he hadn't been three years in arrears with his rent, his landlord would probably have allowed him to stay on.

But the landlord too, was feeling the pinch and, in desperation, had decided to farm the place himself.

Eventually Joe found somewhere to go; a small farm just over the county border, a farm which - like thousands more in the late twenties - couldn't even find a tenant. The owner hadn't been able to find anyone to take it on. Times were bad. Even the 'Farm Sales' advertisements offered three months credit! But with his farm livestock sold to try and meet the demands of the creditors, Joe looked for someone who wanted some livestock boarding out on 'agistment'. In this way he wouldn't need any capital and would receive periodic payments from the various livestock owners. Several of his old friends and former neighbours - including my father - sent him cattle or sheep for the summer. As paying guests!

We were a fairly large family too, and we were having afternoon tea after the only permitted diversion on the Sabbath. We had had a circuitous ride round the country lanes with the pony and trap. Otherwise our Sundays were fairly dull. On a Saturday night Mother would collect all the daily and Saturday papers and put them away, "out of temptation". Naturally we never got a Sunday paper, and we children were always amazed that the old man who delivered Sunday papers in the village wasn't struck down! For years Father never even shaved on a Sunday! (Father's sister, my Aunt Maggie, used to have her Sunday dinner on a Saturday so that there was no cooking to do on the Sunday!) But when a visiting preacher whom Father regarded as little short of being a saint, stayed with us over the Harvest Festival week-end and actually shaved on the Sunday morning Father decided that he could safely follow suit.

The telephone rang! This was a very big event, as it had only recently been installed and we hadn't got over the novelty. A call could be very important. When mother heard the phone ring for the first time, she took her pinafore off before she answered it!

With the public being exhorted at every turn to use the phone more and more, and when even small children seem to have their mobiles, it is maybe difficult to recall those days not so long ago when using the phone simply for a chat wasn't even contemplated. Although my father had the first phone in the village, after the telephone exchange, that is, I cannot ever recall anyone using it simply for a chat. It was nearly twenty years later when I did it!

All through those waiting army years, in the U.K. I had never even thought of the idea of ringing home! Except once. My regiment had moved to the racecourse at Lewes, in Sussex, as we worked our way down to the South coast in preparation for the Normandy landings, and my own Regimental Headquarters section was billeted in the Tote! I had secured a favourite corner position and made down my blankets, when I noticed a dust-covered telephone on the floor. Idly, I took off the handset and was amazed when I heard a brisk female voice saying "Number please!" With rare presence of mind I replied "Trunk Calls, Please" followed by "Lazonby Two, Please!" and in a few moments I was speaking to my mother, to have the first purely social call of my life! At the age of twenty four! Needless to say, the word got round and the relatively small number of gunners whose parents were connected enjoyed free long chats to home. But, back to 1926 and the curious Sunday call.

Father went through into the hall to answer it, although he may have had some doubts about the ethics of so doing on the Sabbath. However he soon returned and carried on with his tea. Mother couldn't restrain her curiosity. "Who was that, Dad?" "It was little Joe", he said. "Well, what did he want?" she enquired anxiously. Normally a man of few words, Father stoically reached for another scone. "You know the sheep I bought last week to send out to Joe's for the summer?" he said. "Well there were a hundred and five altogether. They cost five pounds ten shillings apiece. Well, a hundred and three of them are dead."

Gradually we learned more of the disaster. Father had more than enough grazing for his own livestock, so he had gone to Carlisle mart and bought a hundred and three or four grey-faced gimmer shearlings specially to send to Joe. With luck they might make, maybe ten shillings apiece profit by autumn when they would be sold at 'tupping-time' out of which, of course, he would have to pay the agistment cost. He was probably to regret that he hadn't bought a cottage or two, or even a small street of terrace-houses in Carlisle, for the same money.

Sheep farming mainly consists of a state of war with the innumerable diseases and parasites to which sheep are prone, and, in particular against stomach worms, liver fluke, and parasites. Sometimes *rigor mortis* is the only symptom!

On our farm we had always made a practice of dosing newly bought sheep for stomach worms. It is quite an easy though extremely expensive job nowadays. The alternative of doing nothing is even more expensive. Routine dosing is now carried out by means of calibrated 'dosing guns' which are connected by a tube to a plastic container strapped to the operator's back so that large flocks can be dosed in a very short time.

Father had sent a couple of two-ounce dosing bottles to Joe together with the written formula; "Dissolve one ounce of blue vitriol (Copper Sulphate) in five pints of hot water. When this is cool, each sheep to have two ounces of the solution." (After all these years I can't vouch for the formula! Don't try it!).

But Joe had got his instructions all wrong! Instead of an ounce of copper sulphate, he had mixed a *pound*! Then he had dosed the doomed animals with the lethal mixture. Not quite all. Two sheep had survived! They must have had the good fortune to have somehow been missed. We youngsters knew when to keep quiet. This was one of those times. Father continued with his tea. "What did you say to him?" said Mother, after a long silence. But Father had almost said what he was ever going to say on the matter. As he buttered another scone he said, "I just told him to bury them!"

There was nothing more said for there was nothing to say, and I never, ever, heard him mention it again. But I always suspected that he secretly put it down to divine retribution, because little Joe had done the job on a Sunday!

Chapter 26
Right and Straight

It was Tuesday morning so naturally I was at Penrith Auction (Penrith Farmers and Kidds; sadly no relation!) twenty minutes or so before the weekly dairy sale commenced.This was an important time because I could wander up the lines of cows and ask a few vitally important questions. “Is your cow right and straight in every way, Tom?" "No, Malcolm, its a bit hard to draw on ya hind teat, but she does give a lot of milk." But Tom knew that I wouldn't buy it. Some dealer would do so, and lo and behold, the cow's teat which had been 'hard to draw' would make a miraculous 'recovery'.

Years later at a harvest festival supper the same, but now retired farmer pulled me to one side. 'Dus't remember buying a couple of heifers fra me ya morning at Peeruth aboot twenty year ago?" I couldn't recall it of course, so he refreshed my memory. "Thou knaws, thou alus came round afore t'sale started.Thou asked me about t'heifers 'were they a hundred per cent 'right an straight' an when they cum into't ring thou bowt them beath" he said."But when thou went onto't next chap t'me, an asked him questions aboot his heifer, an thou said 'Is the heifer used to lying in cubicles, or has it been accustomed to being tied up?" T'fella looked a bit capt, an said 'Which sort is't wanten ?'

My wanderings up the line of cattle came to a halt at a group of three Ayrshires. I knew the owner slightly, for I had bought some Ayrshire yearling heifers from him a few months previously. He made a practice of buying in-calf cows from somewhere in Scotland, and selling them after calving. Sometimes, if everything went right he probably made a modest profit on the deal, as well as having a calf of some sort left on his hands to sweeten the transaction. 'What's up Mr Travis?' I asked, for he looked a very unhappy man. 'You'd be a worried man, too', he said, 'if you'd sent six thousand pounds worth of cows to a chap down in Kent, an hadn't got paid!' (This was when one could have bought a new BMW for that amount.)

A good enough reason for looking unhappy. After asking him what sort of routine enquiry he had made, before the deal commenced, I was amazed to find that he had relied entirely on the man's appearance. "Seemed an honest chap, and driving a new car. I never had a doubt about him" he said, sadly. "Said he'd send t'cheque back wid t'lorry driver. The haulage bill alone was £300", he added mournfully.

This was a serious situation."Why don't you go down and get it sorted out?" I asked. It was even more serious than I had thought, for I was pretty sure that Travis, (not his real name) would have bought the in-calf cattle from an auction company on extended credit himself, and would be expected to pay for them when they calved and were saleable.

But he shrank at the prospect of trying to get it sorted out, and I was rash enough to offer to go down to Kent with him to try and salvage something from the debacle. We weren't even on Christian name terms! "Meet me at that lay-by the end of the lane at three o'clock" I said, "and we will see what we can do! But bring a case and some clothes, in case you have to stay for a day or two until the job is cleared up".

But when I had eventually finished my urgent tasks, and picked him up at the rendezvous I was amazed to see that he had no case, but just a rug. "I thought I could just sleep in your car, Mr Kidd." he said, naively. He climbed into my old 'Mark 10' and we set off with all haste to Kent. I broke it to him that there was a possibilty that he might have to put up somewhere for at least a day or two, in the hope that he could firstly, recover the cows - (that is, if they hadn't already been slaughtered and in effect lost without trace) and secondly try and sell them as best he could in the nearest suitable market,in order to save the unnecessary expense of carting them three hundred miles home again.

From this point on, conversation ceased as the windscreen was hit by some flying object and immediately 'frosted' over. I broke enough of a hole to enable me to continue driving. Travis thought that he had better have a hole of his own, and smashed a better one than mine. So until I managed to get an emergency plastic screen somewhere in Bedfordshire, we had a somewhat cold trip.

It was getting almost dark when we found the little Kentish farmstead, almost hidden in picturesque orchards. A short sturdy man came to the door. He reminded me instantly of a well known, -and by the aficionados - a much 'hated' all-in wrestler - Mick something or other. But he asked us in politely and as we sat by the small fire, I began to question him. Although there had been no actual mention of me acting as spokesman, it had been tacitly understood that was why I had made the trip in the first place. 'Mick' cut me short and asked if I had any financial interest in the cattle; which I naturally had to deny, of course. 'In that case' said Mick very gently, 'you'll have to go out'.

There wasn't any choice, so I went out and sat in the car in the dark. After a while I thought I could maybe have a quiet walk round the farmyard buildings and see if there was any sign of Travis's cattle. By now they might all be in carcase form in the East End of London. A dog or two 'gave mouth' and the door opened and I could see Mick peering out into the darkness. Travis told me later that he had said 'If that's Kidd looking round my buildings, I'll break his back!'. Travis didn't doubt that he could do it. By this time however I was sitting innocently in my car.

After about maybe an hour, I awoke, and as Travis showed no sign of emerging, I rapped at the half-open door and shouted "Come on, we're wasting time here!" He joined me in the car and said "There's no joy there, Mr Kidd. What should we do now?" I thought it was quite a good question.

I decided that the first essential was to establish that the cows were still alive and on the premises, and that we might be able to enlist the services of a policeman,in the role of bodyguard. I had an idea that some forces do make men available, for a fee of course, for such eventualities. "We're going straight to Maidstone

Police Station" I said firmly, "to see if we can hire a policeman tommorow morning to go round the farm with us.

At the Police Station however, an inspector listened intently to our story. He pursed his lips and shook his head sadly at the mention of 'Mick', but agreed that, yes, they do hire policemen from time to time for various purposes, but that sadly all their spare men were already hired on this very basis and off to London to 'help' at the Cup-Final! Up to now however, he warned, there was nothing the Law could do. 'No offence had yet been committed' he said! It *could* however happen, it was a possibility that the man would not keep his promise to pay for the cows, in which case the full majesty of the law would swing ponderously into action. But that time was not yet. 'And, by the way Sir, your car is on double yellow lines!'

"Whatever will we do now, Mr Kidd? It's about two o'clock in the morning!" But I was busy perusing the AA Book. "Well, we will have to put up for the night". Bitter experience had taught me that at two o'clock in the morning the only chance of a hotel is to pick one with a three or four 'star' rating. One that has a night porter. And eventually we rang the bell with one such at Rochester about ten miles away. The night porter let us in and showed us to a twin bedded room, and was kind enough to bring me a large whisky. Travis, a member of a strict evangelical sect, looked a bit horrified at this, but divested himself of his boots and lay on the bed and was fast asleep before I had brushed my teeth.

When I awoke, Travis had already gone down, and I found him sitting near a telephone. "I've been on the phone to Judith" he said, "and she says that our solicitor says we have to do nothing!" "Well, are you going to take *his* advice, or mine?" I asked, somewhat testily, "If you are taking other advice, I'll have my breakfast and then I'll be on my way home". "No, no!" said Travis, "I'll take *your* advice". Then after a pause, he said hesitantly, "What is it?" It was another good question.

Suddenly as we ate breakfast I was able to tell him. "I have used a private detective round here some years ago in a difficult case," I said. "If only I can think of his name." Suddenly as we drank our coffee it came to me. In only a few minutes I was speaking to him on the telephone. We might yet be lucky.

"Yes, I have heard of the chap," said the detective, "but I have never actually met him. My Assistant has always dealt with him. He's a former Army heavyweight boxer. Now he serves summonses and so on. When we do that sort of work we are acting as "Officers of the Court" he said. "And this chap has had summonses for years. Never pays more than a few months, pleads poverty or illness and gets away with a few bob a month. Been going on for years. He was jailed once for shooting - although probably well over the fellow's head - at a bailiff".

It seemed that this was the answer to our prayers. The two of them would come with us, and we arranged a rendezvous on the Maidstone by-pass, where we explained our dilemma and arranged the subsequent actions. Our little convoy drew up in front of the farmhouse, and when I was sure we had been seen I got down and passed what looked like a cheque, to Travis, who was sitting in the detectives' car, before rapping firmly on the door. Feeling a bit like Daniel must have done, I entered the house and immediately took the initiative.

"Outside in the other car are two Officers of the Court," I said exactly what I had been told to say, "and you know one of them already! He has been here serving writs on a number of occasions. The other is his senior Officer of the Court. I'm going to call them all in, in a moment, and as I'm now a part owner of the cattle - you probably saw me passing Mr Travis the cheque - I am going to put a proposition to you". With that I went to the door and waved in Travis and the two detectives.

"In the absence of full and immediate payment for these cattle we are seeking your assurance that you will hand them over, with all due care and assistance to transport which will arrive tommorow to pick up them up. In the presence of these witnesses, will you give this undertaking?" I felt sure that I had memorized the phrase correctly, as I looked at Mick for his reply.

"Well, it doesn't look as if I have any option" said Mick rather sullenly. "But the three cows that have calved all had dead calves!" he said. But apart from that, yes, you can pick them up". With that somewhat doubtful assurance we left the room and drove away. A few miles on we pulled up in a lay-by and Travis asked the senior detective for his bill. "Twenty pounds alright?" This was better than Travis had hoped for, so he wrote out a cheque. We all shook hands and then drove our separate ways."It was money well spent" I said, "Now all we have to do is to arrange for the cows to be picked up tommorow".

However there *are* some honest men about and a Dorking cattle dealer whom I knew was in that category, agreed to pick up the cows, take them home, and subsequently sell them on behalf of Travis, as the rest of them calved, and would take any calves and charge £2 a cow for all his services. Travis wasn't in a position to haggle and accepted readily. I paid our bill, filled up the car, yet again, and set off for home. Nearing the rendezvous we rang for Travis to be picked up. Before he got out he asked "What about your expenses, Mr Kidd?" I told him about the petrol and the hotel bill, and said it came to about seventy five pounds. Travis wrote out a cheque, but as he got out he asked me to 'hang on to the cheque for a week or so' before paying it in.

Chapter 27

The Salmon Poacher's Sunday Dinner

If the little stone building had been a bit nearer a road, by now it would have been snapped up by a property developer or by somebody in search of a holiday cottage. But although these odd little stone buildings are rapidly disappearing from the two counties, quite a few still remain. Their mainly inconvenient locations and absurdly small size almost precludes any practical use. They were built in the middle of the nineteenth century when farming was probably in a period of relative affluence. Most of the stone sheds, the 'Hoggests', were say, roughly about the same proportions as a bungalow which might be thought a bit on the small size. These were the sheds in which the hoggs, that is, the ewe lambs which were intended for breeding the following year, would spend the worst of the winter months.

The hoggests had been plonked down just anywhere on the farm and often in quite inconvenient spots which, of course, might have been due simply to the fact that there was a convenient source of building stone nearby. Most of them have, in fact, stood empty for most of the twentieth century, forming quiet havens for pairs of barn owls.

One of the odd little buildings however, was home for old Bill, at least for most of the year. Bill Raine was principally a salmon poacher although it was suspected he could turn his hand to almost any kind of nefarious activity. But he had never had a conviction. But luckily for Bill, in conformity with her religious principles my Aunt Maggie saw to it that Bill at least had a cooked hot Sunday dinner at White House, Glassonby. But it had to be on *Saturdays*, at twelve o'clock precisely!

Bill knew exactly when to turn up. He was there at about five minutes to twelve at White House, where Maggie had lived most of her married life. Every Saturday without fail, he appeared for his Sunday dinner. He seemed to simply materialize. On the Sabbath itself there was nothing done on the farm which could be even remotely described as 'unecessary work'. It was the Sabbath and apart from feeding the livestock there was absolutely nothing done 'which could be done on other days of the week'. Chapel twice a day and being a Sunday School teacher on Sunday afternoons more or less filled Maggie's Sabbath.

So Maggie made the traditional hot Sunday dinner, but she made it on Saturdays instead, so that there was the minimum of cooking on the Sabbath when consequently there was always a cold meal. Tom, her husband, wasn't quite as devout but like thousands of good husbands, went along with her wishes uncomplainingly.

Tom was of an inventive mind and had had a generator installed in one of the outbuildings in the early twenties, more than twenty five years before the village was provided with electricity, and in an otherwise empty building had dozens of large square glass batteries which provided a reserve of more than enough electricity for the house. The laying hens were thus enabled to have electric light provided in their sheds, and confirmed Tom's theory that the bird's laying metabolism was triggered by the total amount of light, albeit artificial light, which they were subjected to during the long dark days of winter. Egg production was a haphazard affair in the early twenties and consequently the supply of eggs almost ceased in winter and any available eggs found a ready market at scarcity prices. Tom could have made a fortune if he had gone into poultry keeping in a really big way.

Bill Raine used to sit in the old tool-shed and eat his hot Sunday dinner; meat of some sort but usually mutton, with ample gravy and two veg, which was usually followed by rice pudding and a pint mug of tea. Maggie hadn't the slightest worry that some of Tom's tools might be missing for she considered Bill as honest as the day. When he took the plates, roughly rinsed in the trough, to the back door he thanked her graciously but without any servility, for her hospitality, and for the last week's copy of the 'Christian Herald' which she gave him in the fervent hope that it might put him on the 'right road'. Bill always thanked her for the dinner with considerable grace, and again for the 'Herald'. She never knew that he couldn't read.

Harold, my brother, was mowing thistles in the Saint Michael's Well field with an old grass-mower. He knew that it wouldn't do much good, for the thistles had already seeded. But it would look rather better, for the field was practically in the middle of a local landowner's land and in fact access to the field could only be gained be exercising one of two old rights of way. One was through the old chap's land and the other was a bit more difficult, it led from the village along the bank of the River Eden and at two quite different locations the actual banks had been washed away in a giant flood.

Consequently access could only be gained by taking the horses and carts through several feet of water. Thus although the right was still there it was difficult to exercise, especially when the river level was high in winter.

Harold became aware of somebody trying to attract his attention in the next field, but one, about a hundred and fifty yards away from where he was mowing. He had to stop the tractor to hear whatever it was the old chap was saying. For it was Old Bill. It seemed urgent. Harold stopped the tractor to enable him to hear the message. "Can thou fetch thi tractor ower here?" He could just manage to make out what seemed to an urgent message. So he hoisted the cutter bar of the Ferguson mower into its upright travelling position and drove up the field a couple of hundred yards, opening and shutting the gates as he went up into the top lane and down again a similar distance through Johnson's field to Bill's hoggest. The whole operation might have taken about a quarter of an hour.

"What's t'want, Bill?" said Harold somewhat irritated, as he realized that there didn't seem anything amiss or any sort of emergency. "What ah want is for thee to run ower mi pillow wid thi tractor!" said Bill firmly. "Run ower thi pillow?" said Harold, understandably annoyed. "Aye!" said Old Bill firmly, "Ah wants thou to run ower mi pillow wid thi tractor. T'pillow's full uv mice an the little buggers chow mi lugs of a neet!"

Obviously under some pressure from the River Eden's riparian owners who felt that their salmon stocks were being unduly depleted by Bill, the matter had reached the point where 'something had to be done'. The first step was to keep Bill under close observation. He had, almost unbelievably, never had a conviction in his life.

A day or two later Bill was seen to emerge from an old and disused barn in Great Salkeld, right into the arms of the law. The village policeman and the Eden Fishery Board water bailiff, had evidently waited in the close vicinity of the barn since dawn. When Bill came out, almost right into their arms, they couldn't believe their luck, for Bill was carrying over his shoulder a weighty looking sack. The two minions of different aspects of the law tried to conceal their elation. Any questioning would only be a formality for Bill's sack bore an evocative curved shape which told its own story. A couple of early risers stopped to see these upholders of the law operating with hitherto unknown efficiency. This was to be a village drama.

"Now Bill! Ah think we've got thou red-handed this time!" said the bailiff with some considerable satisfaction. But Bill said nothing.

The police sergeant cleared his throat. In a way he was sorry that it had come to this, for as a somewhat unsuccessful fisherman himself he had always had a sneaking admiration of Bill's abilities "Now then Bill" he said gently, "the game's up this time! Let's see what thou's got in that bag, if you dont mind, that is', he added. The Water Bailiff started to say something but the policeman stopped him in his tracks. "Bill!" he said,this time quite firmly. After all this was a civil matter, Bailiffs in his view were only glorified gamekeepers. Bill had stopped instantly and waited quietly until the matter of protocol had been sorted out. He still said nothing, and just stood there. Another passer-by stopped to see what was happening."Now Bill" said the policeman firmly.

"Would you mind letting us see what thou's got in that bag?" It was an official but polite request. Proper procedure. Always best.

Bill, still silent, slowly and reluctantly took the sack from his shoulder, and very slowly and deliberately tipped out into the road half a motor-bike tyre.

Chapter 28
The Trophy

My score of salmon in the Parish waters was now a respectable seven. This was largely because I now used a boat. An old boat and a leaky boat, but provided I bailed it out from time to time or whenever it seemed to be riding low in the water, it served my main purpose.This was merely to convey me to a point downstream of the main buttress of the bridge near the deepest part of the river, at least on this stretch.

Over the years several boats were washed away downstream by a sudden rise in the level of the river. There was no permanent mooring, simply a large block of concrete or a large stone attached by twenty or thirty feet of chain to a float. Because of odd incidents of childish vandalism it seemed sensible to keep the boat moored as far from the shore as possible. To retrieve it wasn't quite so simple. A wire grapnel had to be cast out and after several attempts would eventually lodge in the boat and enable it to be pulled to the river bank where it could be bailed out. A year or two before, the bridge had been closed to vehicular traffic for a period of six months or so while strengthening work was undertaken. This was a direct result of the next bridge upstream at Langwathby being washed away in a violent flood round about March of 1968. Accordingly all the historic old bridges were in turn stripped right down to the actual arches, and then restored with reinforced concrete.

I was going off with my tractor to sow swedes one spring morning when I paused for a moment to pass the time of day with my mother who was in her garden; when the water-bailiff whom I knew well pulled up his Land-Rover and shouted "You should be off down to the river! There are five or six big ones just below the bridge!" and he then drove off, leaving me to wrestle with my conscience. Eventually I won, or lost - depending on how you look at it - the uneven contest and drove back home to park the tractor and equip myself with fishing tackle. It probably took all of half an hour before I was driving back down the village to the river.

By the time I had bailed out the boat and then pushed off for the main buttress, some time would have elapsed but it didn't seem long before the bailiff, returning from our market town of Penrith, pulled up on the bridge and peeped over to see how I was doing. Contrary to general belief time simply flies when one is fishing. As I slowly reeled-in my bait, a three inch 'yellow belly', he shouted down to me "You are not deep enough in the water! You need to be at least six feet deeper!" and feeling no doubt that the narrow bridge was no place to be parked he turned to drive away.

Consequently he missed the historic battle, for at that moment I was into a fish. There was no point in shouting to him to watch as he undoubtedly would have done - so I concentrated on my own job which was at all costs to try and prevent the salmon from running upstream through the main arch of Lazonby Bridge. Had it done so there was every chance that it might take the obvious course of shooting down through a different arch which would effectively put paid to my efforts. With one hand I pulled up the 'anchor weight' and held the rope with my teeth until the swift current got hold of the boat and gently swept it downstream followed hesitantly by the salmon. I was then in a position to 'anchor' again and using more conventional tactics eventually take the salmon with the noose of the 'tailer' round the base of his tail. Then I went home to sow my turnips. That fish weighed eighteen pounds.

Eventually Pamela was persuaded, against her better judgement, to come and 'crew' for me and we passed a fruitless couple of hours before finally 'making contact'. We were again in the swift current just below the bridge where the water almost appears to boil. "This is a big one!" I said excitedly as I reeled in loose line and then could feel the enormous pull on the line. "What should I do?" she cried, I couldn't answer for a minute as I was busy keeping the pressure on. I didn't want the line to break if it rubbed against the sandstone arch. The way it was fighting it seemed more like a sea trout of enormous proportions.

Eventually I felt I was in control and Pam directed the open loop of the tailer over the still unseen adversary. I grabbed hold of the handle and brought 'him' close to the side of the boat and gripped it firmly to bring it in. It was indeed a big one. Almost three feet long. Not one to boast about although it now has a proud place in my toolshed for in fact it was a Cumberland County Council shovel hooked half-way along the handle. I still have it.

Jim Scott, a skilled joiner who also ran a well known fishing hotel at Kirkoswald called on my 'services'. One of his clients, a London barrister, had been on a fishing holiday in Norway and had landed an enormous salmon, equal to the English record weight although not quite reaching the tremendous weight of the salmon landed by a 'lady fisherman' in Scotland. There was no way of bringing the fish home, and so he had adopted the old expedient of making a cardboard silhouette and this cardboard had been sent to Jim with the request that he try and make a presentable wooden facsimile salmon to hang in his trophy room. Jim had made a presentable copy of the original fish based on the shape and size of his pattern, from a piece of sycamore. Would I be able to paint the wood in lifelike colours?

In due course I felt satisfied with the result and informed Jim that if he gave it a few days it would be ready to pick-up. But the barrister was to call unexpectedly that night. "No problem, Jim!" I said, "I'll bring it over in half an hour". Yes, the paints were quite dry; the fish was fit to travel. So I popped it in the car to deliver it to Jim. He might conceivably think it was worth a bottle of whisky. As I approached the bridge I could see my old boat at its mooring just below the bridge. But it was dangerously low in the water and I shot off down the little lane to bail out my boat. It only took a few minutes and I was about to let the boat float freely out to the mooring when a visiting angler passed the time of day, and without being asked, showed me his valid Parish Council fishing permit.

Introductions thus being completed I told him about the enormous salmon lying on the back seat of my car. With a humorous gleam in his eye he suggested that I stand in the boat and hold up the

The Trophy - facsimile of the record breaking salmon someone had caught in Norway!

salmon when he would take a photo with his Polaroid camera as a leg pull - which it certainly has been over the years.

At the critical moment a coachload of pensioners came slowly over the narrow hump-back bridge and stopped and all the pensioners debouched onto the bridge to see this once-in-a-lifetime salmon. Several cars stopped to let the drivers look at 'the accident', some coming the other way had to pull up. Horns started to sound as I held up the fish for a few seconds to let the pensioners get a good look at this lovely 'fish', in living colour, and then slowly turned it round so that they could see its white unpainted side.

Chapter 29

Dirty Water and Blue Blood

Entering our village of Lazonby from the west, one sees the biggest cattle watering point for miles around, apart, that is, from the six miles of the west bank of the River Eden, and curiously enough, two small stretches of the eastern bank. One of these near our lovely hump-backed narrow and quite dangerous bridge was fairly obviously caused by a dramatic change in the course of the river. The other bit is more difficult to determine and nobody knows when it occurred.

Until the closing years of the ninteenth century, few villages had piped water, either for man or beast. Until 1893 everybody in the village had to rely on wells for their drinking water. We have a well of our own. Half way down the drive, but now concreted over. But when I excavated it in the fifties, to see if the temperature of the water was low enough to justify the expense of pumping it up to my dairy for milk-cooling purposes, I found that there was no significant difference between its temperature and that of the piped water. So the well was flagged and concreted over again and heavily laden lorries have passed over, unknowingly, ever since. But down there water still runs.

There were about twenty five wells up and down the village, the majority being adjacent to the Harrow Beck which flows down to the Eden from Lazonby Fell. In reality most of them weren't wells at all, in the conventional sense, where the water is wound up to the surface by someone turning a sort of windlass handle.They were simply convenient holes - in some cases only a few yards from the beck - which had been excavated and later tidied up with stone work and sometimes, doors, but the fact remained that they weren't really wells at all in the normal sense. They simply filtered the beck water somewhat as it soaked through the intervening soil.

The water would be crystal clear but full of bacteria of all sorts. One only needs to look round at the headstones in an old churchyard to see how many whole families were almost wiped out at very early ages. In appearance the water would be as clear as crystal. But unless it was chlorinated, this sparkling water wasn't fit to drink. And it still isn't. In spite of the complaints Water Boards continually receive, there are many worse tastes and smells than chlorine! Any Army watercart driver will tell you that.

The peat and sphagnum moss on the great mass of Lazonby Fell, which acted as an enormous reservoir, once held millions of gallons of rain water which was slowly released down Harrow Beck. If the beck had dried up then, as it fairly frequently does in summer nowadays, then the village almost certainly would have been located elsewhere. On many fells and moorland areas - where misguided drainage schemes, which have been encouraged by generous subsidies, or large scale aforestation has taken place- then the becks which used to water the villages simply need no encouragement to dry up. There are no reserves.

The first site where the water was utilised was at "Skinhouse", almost on the side of the road from the West. There only remains a walled sheepwash through which the beck flowed freely except when it was wanted to give the ewes a bit of a clean-up before clipping time. Prior to that it might have been something to do with the old name for the adjacent walled area formerly known as 'Skinhouse'. But it wasn't only the human population which needed water. There was livestock of all sorts. The farms were small and herds of more than ten or fifteen cows were rare. But such farms would probably have two or three horses as well. The sawmill at the bottom of the village had two teams of four horses. To see these powerful animals pulling home their evening loads of huge tree trunks was a splendid sight. At the top of the steep hill in the middle of the village, the waggons had to stop, for there was only a primitive 'braking system. The rear wheels were chocked with renewable wooden wedges, kept on chains for the sole purpose of braking the rear wheels, totally immobilising them. Now huge timber waggons have sophisticated loading cranes which are operated by the driver, and load and cart as much timber in a day as old Forester and Jackson and two teams of horses carted in a week. Progress is often quite sad.

Altogether, the village farms might have a total of more than a hundred cattle and thirty or forty horses, and this livestock constituted an enormous thirst which had to be satisfied twice a day somewhere, but probably most were at Will Pool, the biggest "watering-gap." One can only try and visualize the scene as some sort of order would have to be worked out to avoid mixing the small herds.

The whole site is walled-in on three sides, and has a small grassy area next to the road. The story goes that as we have no village green this spot was chosen to commemorate the coronation of King Edward the 7th by planting an oak tree and two sycamores, together with a suitably inscribed stone. However by the time that action was taken - in the usual way that these decisions seem to be implemented - George the 5th was actually crowned king, so his name is the one on the stone! Edward, in his youth, had been a frequent visitor in the Eden valley, especially to the mansion - long since demolished - at Edenhall and it was said that when Edward or some of his fellow guests had dined and wined rather too well, on occasions a comely little chamber maid or two would find themselves with child.

An old mole catcher was actually quite proud of the royal blood he said flowed through his veins. "Aye, mi father allus said he got two hundred pun t'marry mi muther. It was what awe these big toffs paid when they gat a lass inta bother. It set some of mi mates up fur life. But mi Father allus said he'd ha married mi muther fur nowt!" Praise indeed! And the couple lived a long and productive life in the cottage they bought and furnished for a lot less than the two hundred pounds. Until he shaved off his pointed grey beard Father said there was a remarkable resemblance to the old king.

After the water was piped from Waddigill, on the slopes of the Pennines in 1893, the wells and watering gaps became redundant. Will Pool began to silt up and this process continued until the Second World war when Will Pool and its two "satelites" - which watered livestock, in the next door fields, were cleaned out and were available in case the war touched Lazonby directly and the Auxilliary Fire Service knew they could count on several thousand gallons of water at Will Pool. But fortunately it was never needed.

My father had bought some strong army-surplus First World War ammunition boxes for use as feeding troughs for the fattening bullocks, and I found that two of them - nailed side by side - made a perfectly adequate boat for a small boy. Three of them would carry two boys. But it wasn't easy to get father in the right mood to loan three! These boxes were very stoutly made indeed, for the purpose for which they were originally intended - probably eighteen pounder shells - and were jointed at each corner with mortice and tenon joints. It is likely, or at least possible, that they were of Lignum Vitae for they were exceptionally heavy.

During my first summer holiday from boarding school in Wales, I busied myself in transporting dozens of "loads" of mud and stones and peat, to the middle of the pond in order to make a small island, for the benefit of any ducks which might like to nest there next season. Maybe the island *was* a bit on the small side, for it was about a yard in diameter and only a few inches above the water line. The ducks ignored it. So next year more ammunition boxes were required as father had dismantled the previous years boat. However there were still plenty to be had, but it might be prudent to wait until father had gone to market.

After taking a couple of boxes up to Will Pool on my "bogie" (no boy would be without one!), they were nailed together, side by side in the orthodox fashion, and even had a board nailed to the middle for a seat. Then it was loaded up with more material with which to enlarge the 'island' and I pushed off. It was great to be back in business.

The pack-horse bridge I built in time for my eightieth birthday

It only required a few deft pushes with the pole, and I was at the island. Then it all happened in a few seconds. The dove-tail joints must have dried out since last being used as a boat and water was pouring in! Huge amounts were coming in at each of the corners. As the boat sank completely, I jumped onto the island. Then the island sank! It sank under my weight until its small area was just below the water line. To a casual observer I was walking on water.

There was nobody to be seen, at the nearest end of the village, and I decided that there was no point in shouting. Somebody would turn up before long. But nobody did. I was wet and cold and, I suddenly realized, quite hungry. Boys didn't have watches then. We relied on our stomachs. "It must be dinner time at least!" I thought, "Maybe even tea time? Father wouldn't be back from the market till late. Mother wouldn't be too worried. She would probably think that I'd gone with him." So I just stood there, lonely, wet and cold, and waited. Then, after about half an hour I heard the unmistakable sound of old Holliday's car. Old Holliday was the Vet, although he would have been the first to admit that he had no qualifications. As he drove slowly past Will Pool, I shouted and waved to attract his attention. He obviously had seen me for he waved cheerily back, but didn't stop.

After what seemed an eternity, I saw two of the farm men, who in fact, had just finished their dinners, crossing the stackyard. It was within shouting distance and they came over. After they had finished laughing themselves silly, they returned with the longest ladder on the farm, which enabled me to climb very carefully just above the water, onto one of the surrounding walls.

Years later, when I was chairman of the Parish Council for the first time, I drew the attention of the Annual Parish Meeting to the state of Will Pool. I held up a roughly painted sketch which showed that not only was it almost completely silted up but that it now seemed to be the repository of old buckets and bikes, which I had taken the trouble to emphasize. “That's how it is today, Ladies and Gentlemen". I concluded. "But this is how it could be - very easily!" And I turned over the painting to show the effect of a little work and a small amount of money. There was a cautious but audible murmur of approval, and the Parish Council later agreed to finance the work, "up to a hundred pounds." This small sum enabled the pond to be cleaned out, and bushes and waterside plants soon transformed the site. It so happened that at that time the *Daily Telegraph* and the Ford Motor Company were jointly running the "Save the village pond!" competition and so we entered Will Pool and had the great pleasure of receiving the regional winner's award after a splendid lunch in the River Room at the Savoy Hotel.

The judge's remarks were given when the award was made. He had said that "there were rather too many ducks!" I thanked the organisers for their award, and for organising the public spirited competition, but said that stocking a pool with ducks was a 'fine art. It wasn't an exact science'. We had left the front of the pool unfenced for aesthetic reasons, and the first pair of ducks, which were Mandarins, soon disappeared. Someone gave us a pair of Harlequins which quickly followed the Mandarins into obscurity. So just before the breeding season I bought two pairs of Mallards. They settled down easily, but within a week one of the drakes was run over by a passing car. A week later the female of the other pair followed suit. But the two survivors paired up. So we were still in with a chance. Then the surviving drake was killed and the sole remaining duck cleared off in disgust. She waddled down the lane and disappeared. A month later she returned, proudly leading fifteen lovely little ducklings!

Since then over the years we have had a somewhat more permanent island created, bearing a small flowering crab which promises to be more spectacular each spring. Then for aesthetic reasons alone I built a small stone bridge on the lines of a Lake District pack-horse bridge. Probably the biggest problem with the mallards has been keeping a balance between the sexes, for the drakes seem to prefer to copulate while on the water and such is their sex-drive that a high proportion of the females each year are actually drowned in the act of mating. The waterhens regulate their affairs with much more dignity.

The Lazonby Village Video

One of the objects buried in Lazonby Millennium Capsule was a copy of the 'Village Video', in which Malcolm Kidd attempted to record a full year in the life of the village.

A limited number of copies of this sixty minute video, (with its admittedly quite amateur commentary) is available, price £10.00, post free, from:

Malcolm Kidd
North Bank Farm
Lazonby
Cumderland
CA10 1AJ

A selection of other Capall Bann titles:

The Eildon Tree - Romany Language and Lore by Michael Hoadley

With "A Romany Tapestry" this book forms the most complete (and personal) survey of the Romanies in the 20th century, making the great quantity of material gathered through the author's life available to those with an interest in, and affection for, this unique people. The Eildon Tree" includes traditional Romany tales, Romany phrases and proverbs, songs, sections on a Romany Yule and Samhain and a comprehensive dictionary detailing long-surviving oral tradition which still survives largely as a secret language. ISBN 186163 097 2£9.95

A Romany Tapestry by Michael Hoadley

"Beautifully and honestly written..light and refreshing.." Old Glory magazine

Always interested in alternative lifestyles and alternative medicine, Michael Hoadley started collecting Romany lore and remedies. This book is the result of a lifetime's association with Romany Gypsies, much of it written from a personal point of view. This is a comfortable, fireside book with something to interest everyone - Romany origins, practices, beliefs customs and lore, healing remedies and tales. An intensely personal book about a little-known people who live life to the full in their own very individual ways. ISBN 186163 067 0 £7.95

Crowning Disasters by Yeoman Warder Geoffrey Abbott

As a Yeoman of the Guard (Beefeater) Geoffrey Abbott is well qualified to write books on strange happenings at regal events. The topics covered in this fascinating book range from the hilarious to the unlikely and in some cases quite macabre. Contents include: things that went wrong at coronations, both English and foreign; coronation banquets which frequently ended in chaos, riots and looting; table manners of the day; royal menus; coronation robes and their ultimate fate; used in plays; perks for parasites, favours for flatterers, titles for toadies; flirting and wooing, masques and mistresses, dice-playing, jesters, and other right royal entertainments; regal pretenders and their fate; the English queen tried for witchcraft; coronation medals; duties of the Yeomen of the Guard; attempted assassinations; Napoleon Bonaparte once a London Special Constable! ISBN 186163 1324 £10.95

Gardening For Wildlife by Ron Wilson

"..a real delight...a fascinating read...all of the methods I have tried so far have gleaned superb results" Touchstone ***"lively, colloquial style...quick and easy to read...inspiring and full of helpful tips'*** Place ***"..a nice book...lively drawings which clearly illustrate techniques...covers everything...a good starter book"*** Permaculture Magazine

A few 'modifications' and additions could enhance the value of most gardens for wildlife. That is what this book is all about. It offers practical advice and ideas for improvements and where possible suggests the inclusion of 'extra' features which will support and encourage a rich diversity of plant, insect, bird and animal life. Plants, foods and features are all described in plain English. Everything in this book is explained in straightforward terms to enable anyone to help their local wildlife. ISBN 1 86163 011 5 £10.95

FREE CATALOGUE AVAILABLE